M000290277

K.E.M.

KEEP EVERYTHING MOVING

Letting Adversity Guide You to Destiny

DR. KEMBERLY E. MCKENZIE

Lightning Fast Book Publishing, LLC
P.O. Box 441328
Fort Washington, MD 20744

Stay Connected with Dr. Kemberly E. McKenzie at www.kemberlymckenzie.com.

All rights reserved. No part of this book may be reproduced or transmitted in any form or by any means—electronic, mechanical, photocopying, recording, or otherwise—without written permission from the author, except for the inclusion of brief quotations in a review.

The author of this book provides information for reaching high levels of self-development and creating a healthy perspective when dealing with adversity. The provided information is based on the personal philosophy of the author. The intent is to offer general information that, when applied, will aid the reader in their quest for self-discovery. In the event that you use any of the information in this book, the author and publisher assume no responsibility for your actions.

This is a revised edition of the book. An occurance of slight variations of content on the pages may vary from the original version.

All scripture used in this book is from the King James Version unless otherwise stated.

Copyright © 2014

Dr. Kemberly E. McKenzie, Keep Everything Moving (K.E.M.)

All rights reserved.

ISBN-10: 0-9916682-1-9
ISBN-13: 978-0-9916682-1-2

DEDICATION

I would like to dedicate this book to my parents: Bettie Elizabeth McKenzie and Jessie Lee Hemmingway. This book is also dedicated to my siblings (Verdell Tillery and Frankie Mabry), In-laws, nieces and nephews, especially the twins. I would like to also dedicate this book to the McKenzie/Worthington families. A special dedication goes out to everyone who helped shape my life and created my experiences written in each chapter. Another special dedication goes to those readers who will choose to Keep Everything Moving (K.E.M.). Last but not least, I thank God who endowed me with wisdom, grace and strength to write each page.

CONTENTS

ACKNOWLEDGEMENTS

I would like to acknowledge the great leaders that played a part in my spiritual growth. It was a pleasure to serve either under you or with you;

Pastor Frank D. Tucker – First Baptist Church, Washington, D.C.

Pastor Paul T. Veney – Gospel Tabernacle, Harrisburg, PA

Bishop Gilbert Coleman, Jr. – Freedom Christian Bible Fellowship, Philadelphia, PA

Bishop William Hudson III – Prayer & Faith Outreach Ministries, Chicago, IL

Pastor John Hannah – New Life Covenant Church, Chicago, IL

Pastor Aaron Q. Morrison – Love Fellowship Tabernacle, Lawrenceville, GA

Apostle Travis C. Jennings – The Harvest Tabernacle Church, Lithonia, GA

Tommy Ferrell – Briarlake Baptist Church, Decatur, GA

Jonathan Pretorius – Wesbank Baptist Church, Cape Town, South Africa

Alfred Daniels – Strandfontein Baptist Church, Cape Town, South Africa

FOREWORD

Dr. Kemberly McKenzie pours out her most intimate struggles and reveals the laborious journey to get to freedom!!!

When you cruise throughout the pages of this book, you will cry, laugh and even praise God for His mercy and His everlasting grace.... I totally embrace transparency because it is the power that connects with both seen and unseen audiences. This book is a "slap" in the enemy's face. Simply because what the enemy meant to derail, depress and even destroy, God turns around and uses it to deliver the masses!

I believe this Prophetic work is needed in our society today to encourage individuals that God is able to turn their lives around and bring good out of every negative situation.

The masses are plagued with depression and mental illnesses, which have become serious issues. We need more literature that fosters encouragement and mobilization.

Dr. McKenzie encourages the reader to "Keep Everything Moving." My name is Apostle Travis C. Jennings and I approve this book!!!!!

PREFACE

Often times when you have been through horrible experiences, whether your fault or otherwise, you think that everything is okay because you are able to function on a day-to-day basis. You do not realize that those experiences are the undercurrent to your present behaviors and actions. There are some experiences that open the door for certain spirits to attach themselves to us, without our full knowledge or understanding. Not only that, but we operate in some spirits that came down through our bloodlines. Just as cancer, diabetes, sickle cell anemia, etc…, can be inherited in the natural, so it is with certain behavior patterns in the spirit: alcoholism, poverty, rebellion— just to name a few. We walk through life carrying hurts and pains from our childhood and past which plays a role in our environmental coding. Before we know it, we are acting in ways that do not line up with our intended purposes in life with no explanation as to why. That once was me.

Having experienced molestation, sexual assault, rape and several other unwarranted events in life, with no full understanding of the implications behind them, I found myself in adulthood wrestling with unwelcomed spirits that attached themselves to me: Rejection & Rebellion. Eventually they invited their relatives: pride, perversion, self-pity and self-rejection. Before I knew it, I was waddling in the spirits of low self-esteem, regret, anger, bitterness and loneliness. If I had known then, what I know now.

Praise God that through each of these events, He did not allow me to be overtaken to the point of no return. True, I had the experiences, but God still shielded me. I came to a point where I can be transparent and share my testimony. In this, I hope to free others who have had similar experiences. Although my testimony is mainly to help free women from the many traps set up to cause us to not see ourselves as God sees us, this book is for anyone who struggles with any type of spirit(s) or bondage(s). This is not so much about women or men or their relationships; rather it is about being made whole. By the way, spirits know no gender.

Although I share a lot about my hardships in life, this does not negate the fact that God has been good to Kemberly Elaine McKenzie. I lived a blessed life the more because of what I have experienced and endured. This is not my entire life's story; however, it is a snippet into the processes that we, as believers, may go through to get to that rose that God intended for us to become. As you read my story, do not cry for me. I am no longer that wounded, bleeding soldier on the battlefield. I have moved from the infirmary. I have been made whole. I found outer strength for my inner struggles because I learned to celebrate adversity and to use it as a guide to my destiny.

This book was written with you in mind. This book was written to push you into purpose and/or guide you a few steps closer towards destiny. Imagine all of the zillions of people that lived on this earth; not one of them has your foot or fingerprints. What does that say about you? You are an original. You have your own unique path to walk out and process to go through. This includes facing adverse situations throughout your life. Nonetheless, you must believe that you are worth more to God than the flowers, trees, birds and other animals on this planet (Psalms 8 and Matthew 6:26-34).

You are still breathing because God has a purpose and a plan for your life. If that were not the case, He could have snuffed you out of here while you were dead in your sin. "But God Commendeth His love towards us, in that, while we were yet sinners, Christ died for us." Christ died so that we may live. We owe Him our lives. If you have not already done so, now is the time to find out what your purpose is. If you already know and are operating in it: 1) Do not stop when all odds are against you. Keep in mind, you will not get the juice if you do not squeeze the fruit; 2) Reach back and grab or push others toward destiny. The strong should bear the infirmities of the weak, and not to please ourselves (Romans 15:11). After all Jesus is praying for us in our adversities: "And the Lord said, Simon (put your name here), Simon (put your name here), behold, Satan hath desired to have you, that he may sift you as wheat: But I have prayed for thee, that thy faith fail not: and when thou art converted, strengthen thy brethren" (Luke 22:31-32). After you have been rescued, turn around and rescue others.

Allow God to fully heal you of any lingering hurts, pains, embarrassments, shames, guilt and the like so that you, too, can K.E.M. (Keep Everything Moving). Receive the ministry of reconciliation. I admonish you, as you read this book, if you are stuck, regardless as to what it may be, allow the spirit and power of God to set you free. There is humor, healing and deliverance in each chapter for you. Ready, Set, Read!

Chapter 1

DECEPTION AND PERCEPTION

The devil has an objective for us. He persecutes us by instilling guilt and negative thoughts, induced through evocative inner dialogue from the twins: deception and perception. I missed the mark throughout my lifetime because of those twins. It is imperative that we understand how the devil works in our lives. He is subtle and clever. He manages to get his way through manipulation and other methods. He likes to misrepresent the truth by mixing half-truths with lies in order to draw us in to his world. Because, we have access to the plan of salvation: forgiveness for our sins, fuels the devil's anger since he no longer has this privilege. Every day humans wake up to new mercies. Unfortunately for the devil, that is not his case. He will never be forgiven.

DECEPTION

Have you ever wondered how magicians are able to fool us with their magic tricks? The reason being, magicians know how people in their audiences think. Most humans process the world through homogeneous lenses. Homogeneous means to be similar in nature;

uniform. This means that for the most part, people have similar ways of processing. However, there are exceptions of a few who dare to think outside the box. Looking at life through this type of lens, allows others, such as magicians, to easily influence us, in order to fool us into seeing exactly what they want us to see. This is also how the enemy uses deception to trick us as well.

Because of our homogeneous lens, the enemy is able to bend reality in order to completely fool us into believing his lies like the following: I am nothing. God cannot truly love me because my life is a mess. I am unworthy. I am in too deep and will never be able to get out of this.

Satan works hard to convince us of half-truths. Furthermore, he wants to bend the truth of reality to make us think that God is not who He says He is and will not do what He said He would do concerning our individual and collective lives. I fell into this trap. Fortunately, "God is not a man, that He should lie; neither the son of man, that he should repent hath He said, and shall He not do it? Or hath He spoken, and shall He not make it good" (Numbers 23:19)? He watches over His word to perform it. (Jeremiah 1:12b). To the contrary, the devil is the father of all lies, meaning: deceiver (John 8:44). Before going any further, the word deception needs defining. Deception is an act or statement intended to make a person believe something that is not true. Deception is further defined as:

1. Practice of misleading somebody: the practice of deliberately making somebody believe things that are not true
2. Something intended to mislead somebody: an act, trick, or device intended to deceive or mislead somebody.

Magic is all about deception and so is our adversary. Magic tricks are not in the magician's ability to fool us; rather, it is our perception that does the deceiving. Our perception becomes our reality. **The bending of reality is all it takes to be fooled, deceived and/or duped. This deception does not take place externally, but internally.** Again, **the illusion of magic does not rest within the magician, but is embedded in the conformed ignorance of the audience or individual for that matter. We think that the devil is deceiving us when in actuality, we are deceiving ourselves.** That does not negate the fact that the devil is a deceiver any more than the magician being an illusionist. Deception is the vehicle that is used to get us stuck in our past hurts, pains and problems. We deceive ourselves through 1) ignorance and 2) conformity.

Ignorance – The Bible states in Hosea 4:6a, "My people are destroyed for lack of knowledge..." We lack knowledge of who God is. Therefore, we are ignorant. Once we get a revelation of who God is, we can get a revelation of who we are. This minimizes our chances of being deceived by the devil. The Word of God reads, "Lest Satan should get an advantage of us; for we are not ignorant of the enemy's devices," (2 Corinthians 2:11). You see, when we know what we can do and what God can do through us, we can act offensively in tearing down false strongholds and realities within our minds. This brings me to the next point.

Conforming – Romans 12:2 reminds us to "be not conformed to this world; but be ye transformed by the renewing of your mind, that ye may prove what is that good and acceptable, and perfect will of God." We also deceive ourselves through conformity. In this, I mean traditionalism and/or orthodoxy. These are what are known as accepted views and beliefs of the world: prevailing attitudes, if you will. There is a saying, "I believe, therefore, I am." Although Descartes was really proving his existence when he coined this phrase, the Bible does state that "As a man thinketh, so is he" (Proverbs 23:7).

What do you believe about yourself? What do you believe about your life? What do you believe about your present circumstance and condition? What do you think about your past mistakes, misunderstandings and misadventures? Do you think or believe they define you and your future? If you believe the worst about these events and experiences as I did, then you are clearly walking in deception. **The devil, like the magician, can only present the trick or illusion;** however, it is up to us to make the decision to believe the status quo. The bottom line is this; it is up to us as individuals to decide whether or not to believe the lies about our pasts or perhaps our presents.

Yes, according to tradition, if you are a liar, you will always be a liar. Traditionally, it is known that, "once a thief, always a thief." Society deems that if no one in your family owns anything, you will not own anything either. That is deception in its highest form. That example demonstrates how conformity of our ways of thinking can be used to deceive us when viewing our life through homogeneous lens: "I can't do this because I have never done this before or it has never been done." However, know that it is an illusion before putting God into the equation.

God as a Mathematician - Although the devil acts like a magician, God is a mathematician. God uses math to operate in our lives to show and remind us of who He is. He also uses math to show what our past and/or present circumstances are not. He uses inequalities, which are statements that compare expressions, by using the following signs: (< less than), (> greater than), ($\leq$ less than or equal to), ($\geq$ greater than or equal to) and ($\neq$ not equal to). He uses the previous signs to teach us that **Our Problems < Us < God**. This means that our problems are less than us and we are less than God. Therefore, God is greater than both us and our problems.

We can also use improper fractions to illustrate God as a mathematician. An improper fraction is a fraction that has a top number (the numerator) larger than the bottom number (the denominator—9/2). In other words, an improper fraction is top heavy, if you will. In God's math:

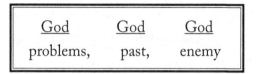

He is over our problems. God is over our past. God is over the enemy. "…Greater is He that is within you, than he that is in the world" (I John 4:4b). For that reason, if God is in me through the working of the Holy Spirit, and He is greater than any/all of my problems (past and the enemy) then I, too, am greater than all of these as well. In math, this would be considered a form of reasoning. Inductive or deductive reasoning are two methods of logic used to arrive at a conclusion based on information assumed to be true. They both can be used in research to establish hypotheses.

Inductive reasoning – It is the process of arriving at a conclusion based on a set of observations. However, it is not necessarily a valid means of truth. Because a pattern has been derived from a number of situations, does not make that pattern true for all situations. For example, the first 20 people that walk through the door either were wet or had umbrellas that were wet. You perhaps assume it is raining outside. However, after going outside, you noticed that in order to get into the building, people had to walk past the automatic sprinkler system. Inductively, one could reason that it is raining outside and it very well may be. Nonetheless, in this instance, that was not the case.

Deductive reasoning - On the other hand, this is a valid form of proof. It is the process by which conclusions are made based on previously known facts. For example, previously when I stated that we are greater/bigger than our past, problems and enemy because of God, demonstrates a form of deductive reasoning. It is a step-by-step process of drawing conclusions based on previously known truths. To further break down the point I am trying to make regarding deductive reasoning, typically, a general statement is made about an entire class of things and then a single example is given.

If the example fits into the class of things formerly mentioned, deductive reasoning can be used: if God is greater than my past, problems and enemy and God's spirit resides in me, I am greater than my past, problems and enemy. In this instance, deductive reasoning works out, but there are times when it does not. In those instances, that is what I call a toe hole. A toe hole is a point by which deception enters our minds. By the way, a toe hole becomes a foot hole and a foot hole in turn becomes a stronghold. A stronghold is defined by Webster as a place that has been secured tightly or a place where a particular belief or ideology is firmly believed and staunchly defended. "For the weapons of our warfare are not carnal, but mighty through God to the pulling down of strongholds; Casting down imaginations and every high thing that exalteth itself against the knowledge of God and bringing into captivity every thought to the obedience of Christ" (II Corinthians 10:4-5). Imaginations are the formation of a mental image of something that is neither perceived as real nor present to the senses.

In the New International Version (NIV) this same passage of scripture reads, "We demolish arguments and pretension... The definition for arguments is, philosophies, reasoning and schemes of the world. Pretentions have to do with anything proud, man-centered and self-confident. When deductive reasoning does not work, this leads to faulty conclusions. This happens because the assertions were incorrect. Once that thought got in by way of a toe hole, instead of aborting the idea, we pondered over it and allow it to become a stronghold (deception).

It is logical that your great-great grandparents were broke. Your great-grand parents were broke. Your grandparents were broke and your parents were broke. By deductive reasoning, you, too, should be broke. However, you chose to stand on the word of God and declare that wealth and riches are yours. You begin to profess that you are the head and not the tail; the lender and not the borrower; above only and not beneath. On the contrary, if you are not broke, you are prosperous. Deductive reasoning goes like this: everybody that came through your bloodline from your parents on back dealt with the spirit of poverty and passed that spirit on to you. Therefore, we can deduce that you are broke and live in poverty as well. However, God may have chosen to use you to break the cycle of poverty in your family and you are bountifully rich.

The premises used in deductive reasoning are, in many ways, the most important part of the entire process of deductive reasoning. If they are incorrect, the foundation of the whole line of reasoning is faulty and nothing can be reliably concluded. Even if just one conclusion is incorrect, every conclusion thereafter is unreliable and may very well be incorrect also. This leads to deception.

At the age of six I was molested. In college, I was sexually assaulted. Later, in my early young adulthood, I was raped. Growing up, because of my dark complexion and the amount of whippings I received, more than my brother and sister combined, I felt like the black sheep of my family. Statistically, my life should not have amounted to a hill of beans because I was what society considered 'a victim.' Nonetheless, in God's mathematics, I am a better person because of the pain, the problems, the past and the process. Mathematically: Victimization=Victory; Molestation=Ministry and Past (failures+Pain)+Problems=Purpose.

Having said all of this, it is totally up to you how you are going to perceive your life. **Are you going to believe the devil's deception or God's reality?** I did for a long time. I had to learn the hard way, but hopefully in reading this book, you will learn the easy way that **you are who God says you are despite what you have been through or chosen to be.** So what if you are a stripper, a liar, a murderer, a gangbanger, an alcoholic, drug dealer/addict, gossiper, cheater, rebellious or rejected; whether you have accepted Jesus Christ as your Lord and personal savior or not, you belong to God. He is your creator. When God made man out of the dust from the ground, He breathed into his nostrils the breath of life; and man became a living soul. When God finished with creation, humankind included, He looked at His work and said, **"It is Good."**

I earned my 1st masters in 1996, my 2nd masters in 2002, and my 3rd masters in 2005. That was not the end of my story. I obtained my PhD in 2009. This was a great success considering, but what if I had gotten stuck there in the celebration of Dr. Kemberly Elaine McKenzie? I would have never been able to move on to the next: Licensed and ordained Minister Kemberly Elaine McKenzie. I would have never traveled to Cape Town, South Africa, as a missionary to feed and clothe thousands of children. I may have never become, author and motivational speaker, Kemberly Elaine, McKenzie. It is all in how we perceive things. We go from glory to glory.

PERCEPTION

Your perception becomes your reality. Perception: an attitude or understanding based on what is observed or thought. Other words for perception are view or picture. Reality: all that exists or happens; everything that actually does or could exist or happen in real life. Synonyms for reality are: truth, certainty and authenticity. Therefore, if we were to restate the opening sentence we could say your view/picture, becomes your truth/certainty. Therefore, how you view things determines your beliefs. Again, going back to the homogeneous lenses, **your perception has everything to do with how the devil deceives you.** We can no longer accept the devil's lies for truth, but to see him and what he presents to us as a lie. If you know it to be a lie, that becomes your reality and you will not receive or believe anything from him. Contrary to this, **if you start believing that the Word of God is true and only true, that becomes your reality in which you base your standards for living and your decision-making process.** Life will become a lot easier with bad decisions.

All the devil really wants to do is to get you to deny your own testimony as he did me. Then, you would be afraid to share the Love of Christ with others. However, I no longer have to accept fear as a reality because the Word of God says, "For God hath not given us the spirit of fear; but of power, and of love, and of a sound mind" (I Timothy 1:7). I can be bold and courageous in all of my endeavors. The word *fear* in the text is not the fear that we are familiar with in terms of phobias. Rather, in the original Greek language, the word *deilias* is used. This word means cowardice. In essence, God has not given us a spirit of cowardice when it comes to spreading the good news. In the context of I Timothy 1:7, it really is referring to sharing the workload of spreading the gospel that the gift of salvation is free to all. Now that I no longer operate in fear of exposure of my past, I am free to share with others so that they too can know and experience the love of Christ at another level.

Do you usually see the glass as half-full or half-empty? Do you usually see your problems as painful or part of the process for God to get the glory out of your life? **How do you view your life?** How do you view your present circumstance(s)? Can you see yourself above your situation and circumstance? Do you see yourself as greater than your problem and pain? Do you see whatever you are going through as the end all to be all? **What do you see? Your perception becomes your reality.** Do not let deception become your view, your picture. Again, greater is He that is in you than he that is in the world. You are more than a conqueror through Him that loved you.

When you think about the glass situation, it is really a competition between optimism and pessimism. What type of person are you? Your perception determines that. Although you may see and/or understand the purpose in everything, can you see any good coming out of it? For example, if you can see the glass as half-full, then that gives you a starting point. It gives you something to work with. However, to view the glass as half empty is actually pretty comical. Think about it: empty means not containing or holding anything; unoccupied; without value, meaning or purpose. Therefore, in actuality, the glass cannot be half-empty because that means half of nothing. And, nothing from nothing leaves nothing. (Kemberly is singing....you got to have something if you want to be with me... sorry, I went there).

When you perceived the glass as being half-full, you are putting the focus on what is in the glass, what you do have. On the other hand, when you focus on half-empty, you put the focus on what you do not have, what you wished you had or what you want. That is where those twins, perception and deception come into play. **Deception brings the thought and perception carries the thought out**. For example, you may look at the fact that you do not have money for something. Deception paints the picture of all the things you do not have and all the things you want and cannot get.

Perception comes and now your view of yourself is that you are poor/broke. It will never show you that on your salary—you pay a mortgage, a car note, car insurance, student loans, groceries, utilities and feed and clothe five children etc... When you add all that up, you have spent over $3,500 in one month. That is not including the incidentals. So here, the twins have you believing that you are broke, busted and disgusted having nothing, but according to your bank statement and checkbook, you had something. If not you would not have been able to pay your bills, tithes and offering (for some of us) off of nothing: $0. Again, how do you view your life and situation, ½ full or ½ empty?

The devil uses deception and perception to bend back the truth and/or reality if we give him access to our mind. He knows all of our weaknesses and who is more vulnerable to different types of sins or behaviors. Some of it is by way of our bloodline. However, you do not have to be overtaken by the twins of deception and perception. Just like the enemy is working against us, God is working for us on our behalves 24/7. "He that keepeth Israel never slumbers nor sleeps" (Psalm 30:5). He left us with a comforter (Holy Spirit) to lead and guide us into all truth (John 14:26-27).

THOUGHTS TO PONDER

- ❖ Perception is real, but it is not always the truth
- ❖ Use what is in your hand
- ❖ Don't let your mind play tricks on you
- ❖ Check your vision
- ❖ If you change your perception, you change your reality

NOTES OF INSPIRATION

_____

_____

_____

_____

_____

_____

_____

_____

_____

_____

_____

_____

_____

_____

_____

_____

_____

Chapter 2

BIRTH AND DEATH CERTIFICATES

Before I formed thee in the belly, I knew thee; and before thou camest forth out of the womb I sanctified thee, and I ordained thee a prophet unto the nations – Jeremiah 1:5

BIRTH CERTIFICATE

I was called before I was ever born. For that reason alone I have been on the enemy's hit list. As a baby, I was sickly. I would get these fevers and my mom would have to take me to the emergency room in what seemed like every other night. At one point, they diagnosed me with meningitis. However, it turned out that I had problems with my ears. I eventually had surgery on my ears. From that point on I was not able to get water in my ears. Also, flying became quite painful for me as well.

I began talking at 5 months and walking by 9 months. Around 12 months, I fell down the steps at the babysitter's house in a walker. Even then, God had his hands on my life. I was okay, or that may be why I am a clown now. I remember being in the car with my mother around eleven years of age. We were coming from the laundry mat. We were going down a hill and hit an ice patch. The car spun around three times and stopped, facing the edge of a hill. Angels stopped our car from going over that hill. At the time I thought nothing of it. I just remember my mother yelling, "Jesus," while, I yelled, "Mom." I just knew we were going over that hill. That is why one of my favorite songs today is *Just Another Day That The Lord Has Kept Me.*

It was evident then that my birth certificate was a death certificate or shall I say, more like a death warrant. I was a threat. The devil knew that my mom was birthing greatness into the earth. He knew that I was a mover and shaker. Despite what I have been through, I am called and the beloved of God. **I am not perfect but being perfected, daily.**

DEATH CERTIFICATE

The first day on my first job out of college in Philadelphia, I was riding with my supervisor to a meeting. We were in a three-car accident. A car hit the car behind us who in turned rammed into the back of us. One Easter Sunday, my sister, cousins and I were coming from the zoo. I was driving; I pulled up to a stop sign. A woman was driving behind us. She had been drinking and ran smack-dab into the back of us and then tried to say we hit her. Go figure.

While living in Chicago, one of my church members asked me to give her daughter and grandson a ride up the street. She did not have a car seat so initially I said no. She explained that the car seat was at the daughter's house, which was only three blocks away. Therefore, I made her and the grandson sit in the back seat. He was about 2-3 years old. She sat him on her lap and they shared a seat belt. There were six of us in the car altogether. We were driving down the street. As we were approaching an intersection, we had the right of way while the traffic to the left and right had a stop sign. There was a car at the stop sign on my right. A car pulled out from behind that car, drove into the intersection and hit my car at the rear passenger side. This is where the young woman and her son were sitting.

My car was knocked into the opposing traffic lanes where oncoming traffic was approaching us. The street was on an angle. My friend, Ivy, started rocking back and forth while praying/singing: "Oh Jesus; Lily of the valley, Jesus. Bright and morning star, Jesus." My now deceased friend, Jocelyn, started fussing and cussing. The impact was so hard that somehow, the baby was knocked out of the mother's lap and thrown across the car. We all ended up in the emergency room that evening. Again, the woman tried to blame the accident on us, when we were already in the intersection and had no stop sign like she did. She died before we could settle.

In February 2009, I had the 4th knee surgery on my right knee. In March, we were on our way to therapy when a car made a left hand turn in front of us without yielding. Because I was still on crutches, I was sitting in the back seat with my back against the door behind my driver. My legs were going across the seat. The next thing I knew, I heard my driver yell, "Oh, no." I was thrown from the back seat, flipped upside down and thrown into the windshield. My face landed sideways into the glass. I broke the headrest on the passenger side, the console, the rear view mirror and cracked the windshield. I was so disoriented that when the police and ambulance arrived and were asking me what happened, I kept saying that I was thrown into the trunk.

Because of the gifts, talents, anointing and call on my life, the enemy had a plot to destroy me from birth. Psalms 97:10 reads, "Ye that love the Lord, hate evil: He preserveth the souls of His saints; He delivereth them out of the hand of the wicked." The word, preserveth in Hebrew means to place a hedge about (as with thorns), i.e. guard to protect, attend to, etc.: —beware, be circumspect, take heed, mark, look narrowly, observe, preserve, regard, reserve, watch (man). I can say without a shadow of doubt that on March 18, 2009, God protected me. Not only that, but the enemy had to get permission to even attempt to touch me. I hear God saying as with Job, "Go ahead, do what you want, just do not take her life. She can handle it. Watch Me get the glory out of her life."

Not only did my birth certificate become my death certificate in the sense of the enemy laying deadly traps for me. Over the years, I had to learn to die to myself. Sure, all that I have gone through over the course of my life in which you are about to read, taught me to die to this flesh. The flesh loves payback and revenge. I assure you I can come up with ways to pay people back, but that is not God's will for my life, or yours. He said that vengeance is His and He will repay. I once heard a pastor preach that scripture. Instead of coming from a place of God will pay the person back for what they did to you, he said that scripture was punctuated in the original language to mean that God is the avenger. He will repay. However, it is not your enemy that gets repaid; rather, it is you. He pays you back for all that you had to go through and endure. That is why I can write this book, now, with no regrets. I have learned to live and forgive. Why? It is simple; because I was forgiven. A man named Jesus laid down His life for me.

If I had my way, I would be married by now with 12 children. I use to say that I was going to build an army for the Lord. However, you know, that was in my younger days. Now it is just let me have my twins and Keep Everything Moving (K.E.M.). Over time, I came to grips with the fact that God did not want me to be married and have children before now. If so, there were many opportunities He could have allowed that to take place. When I say He knows what is best for you; believe me. I did not need a family then. I was too hurt and bitter back then. I could have destroyed a man with my tongue and actions. You know, **'wounded people wound.'**

In addition to that, I had to come against all the generational curses in my bloodline so that they would not get passed down to my posterity. Now that I have been gutted out, God can trust me with a family. Every man that I set my eyes on or that sat their eyes on me, God said, "No." I could not understand it then, but certainly understand it now. He kept me from having a relationship with my husband behind bars. He kept me from being a battered wife. He kept me from dealing with infidelity. These were the types of men I dealt with in my past.

As badly as I loved and wanted each of those men; He knew what was best for me. This one person in particular, I knew he loved my dirty socks. I loved him back just because of that. God kept telling me that we were unequally yoked. I called myself going to out-smart God and did a study on what unequally yoked truly meant. I was trying to find a loophole in order to stay with this man. At the end of the day, God gave me an Abraham experience. He asked me what if the very thing, or promise, that I had believed Him for and waited on for years, what if He asked me to give it up? I remember lying in my guest room on the floor in a fetal position, crying out to God, but telling Him "yes" at the same time. I did not understand it at the time.

It hurt like crazy. However, what I did know was that God's will was what I wanted for my life and that my birth certificate was truly my death certificate. I had to die to what I had been expecting all of these years. However, the Word of God reads: "They that hope in the Lord will not be disappointed" (Isaiah 49:23). **It hurt then, but in retrospect, it was worth it.** That man ended up going to jail a few times and ended up on drugs. God knows what is best for our lives and when it is best for us as well. Just trust Him and K.E.M. (Keep Everything Moving).

THOUGHTS TO PONDER

❖ You are on a hit list. Get over it
❖ There is a hedge of protection around you; the devil can only go so far
❖ There is life after death once you die to flesh
❖ The devil cannot kill what God wants to live

NOTES OF INSPIRATION

_____
_____
_____
_____
_____
_____
_____
_____
_____
_____
_____
_____
_____
_____
_____
_____
_____

Chapter 3

MISHANDLE AND MISTREATED

Often times we go throughout life blaming ourselves for things and events that took place in our lives that we had nothing to do with. There is a familiar saying, "if I knew then what I know now." If I knew then that all the hell that I had been through from a little girl until now, would make me the person I am today, and my life would be a blessing to others; I would have looked at and perceived my life differently. Instead, I walked in deception and the devil's lies for years believing that my life was a mistake and that I was cursed. I loved the Lord, served in ministry, traveled around the world and even preached His word, but felt unloved and abandoned by God because of my bad experiences and rough life.

I even blamed God when I was the one who made bad decisions at times. I felt that He was God, the one in charge. His word says, "His sheep know His voice." I thought I was a sheep, but I guess I was blind, deaf and dumb because I made what I thought was a complete mess of my life. Who would have known that my mess was my ministry? It took years, upon years, upon years, upon years, for me to stop believing the devil's lie and deceiving myself that I was a big black mistake and my life was one big bad curse and nightmare.

When I allowed God's word to change my mind, it changed my heart. When it changed my heart, it changed my perspective. When I changed my perspective, it changed my life.

Ever since I was a little girl I always felt like the black sheep of the family and of my neighborhood. My brother gave me the nickname T.B. for Tar Bear. For those who dared to have to get in a fight with me, they commenced to calling me that as well. My sister and brother were 9 and 8 years older than me. They got to do more than I did and I always felt my mother was W-A-Y too strict on me; much more than she was with them. I got a beaten for just waking up in the morning (Bettie is going to kill me when she reads this book). Because my mother was so hard on me, us, I thought she did not like me. That spirit of rejection gripped me straight out of my mother's womb. It was not until I got to college that the Lord showed me that my mother raised us the best way she could. She raised us so that we would have a future. Not just any future, but a future in God. She put the fear of God down in me. Well actually, it was the fear of Bettie. I did not understand at the time that God gave me to her to protect my anointing. Her strictness kept me out of a lot of trouble. I did not do a lot of things growing up because I feared my mother not God. I remember her telling me if I ever got pregnant she would make me eat that baby. Now how that was supposed to happen, I do not know, but with Bettie, things like that were possible; or shall I say, I believed they were possible.

MISHANDLED

I grew up in Belford Towers. We had three different buildings: North, East and West. I lived in the East building apt. 110. We were all bused to school. When I went to first grade, I believe my brother was in his last year of junior high school and my sister was in her first year of high school. Their buses came earlier than the elementary school's bus so I had to go to the babysitter until it was time for my bus to come. Some mornings I would go back to sleep once I got to her house. Other mornings, if I were lucky, she would let me watch Captain Kangaroo. I am dating myself now. Anyway, my babysitter loved to watch the news. At six years old, the news was a death sentence. Anyway, my babysitter had a son who was probably somewhere in his early 20's. He would let me come to his room and watch cartoons from time to time. That was a treat until one day he mishandled me.

According to Webster, mishandle means the following: 1) To deal with something or somebody in an incompetent or ineffective way; 2) To treat something or somebody roughly. Synonyms for mishandle are mess up, make a mess of, botch, spoil, ruin or damage. After being mishandled I thought I was ruined, spoiled, and/or damaged. Although I did not quite know at that time that I was 'molested,' I knew that something happened that should not have happened. I remember his long nails scratching my insides and remember how much it burned when I had to urinate. On the contrary, something in me was drawn to it. As painful as it was something in me kind of liked it. Some mornings I was tired and preferred to go back to sleep over watching cartoons, but since he would come and summon me back, I was afraid not to go because he had threatened that I better not tell a soul.

From this experience I was frightened and grew to hate myself over the years for allowing this to happen to me and kind of liking it at the same time. As I got older and recalled what happened to me, I always believed something was wrong with me because I kind of liked something that I should not have and which was painful for me. It was not until years later in my adult life that I learned about the spirit of perversion which can be passed down through our bloodlines. Once that door was open, it allowed me to have an appetite for things. It appeared as if I became a magnet for this type of activity later down the road.

MISTREATED

During college, I failed a class. I had to re-take it in summer school. I took it as an independent study with one of the professors. I attended a private Christian Liberal Arts College and we were a tight community. Many students even called the professors by their first names. Anyway, my professor was over a Boy Scout troop. His family had gone on vacation and he was to catch up with them and the troop later. He stayed back to teach the final week of class and to administer my final exam. I cannot remember all of the details, but for some reason he needed to get a second car home. He asked if I would help him and he would bring me back to campus. I was, like sure. I thought nothing of it. At that particular college, going to a professor's home was nothing. We went over our professors' houses all the time. We got to his house and he invited me inside his house. Still I am not thinking anything because 1) he was a Christian; 2) a professor, 3) married and 4) looked like the dad from *Revenge of the Nerds*.

I went inside his house. He offered lemonade. I saw he had a piano. While he was getting the lemonade, I asked him if he cared if I played the piano. He gave me permission to play. I sat down and played a classical piece. As I was playing he brought the lemonade out and put his hands on my shoulders. He said that I was tense. I asked him what he was doing and to get his hands off me. Next thing I know this man is trying to fondle my breast and then some. I told him to stop and to please take me back to school. We ended up fighting a little bit. For some reason, to this day I do not remember all the details, but I do remember feeling violated although he did not rape me. Now I had sexual assault to add to my already confused molested self.

We got back to campus and I had to work that particular day. I went to work and I was not myself. My supervisor picked up on it and asked me what was going on. I just burst out in tears. He finally got it out of me and I told him what had happened. Of course he could not believe that one of the professors would try such a thing. He encouraged me to call the police; however, I was scared. Where I went to school, there were rumors that the Klux, Klux, Klan met right down the street. I was scared that once the story got out, it would not be what this Caucasian man did to me, but what this little African-American girl allowed to happen to her. I sincerely feared for my life. I called home and told somebody what had happened, but I pretended like it had happen to a friend, and my friend wanted to know what to do about the situation considering where we attended school. The person's response was, "If somebody allows something like that to happen to them and they do not report it, then they wanted it to happen to them." I hung up the phone, confused. I just lay in my bed balled up in a fetal position and just cried the rest of the night away.

It was that night that I began to think back to being molested and the same thoughts came back to mind. I began to blame myself once again. I kept replaying what had happened in my mind over and over again and thinking, what could I have done differently? This time I did not enjoy it, I actually had to fight and push the man off of me. I had totally forgotten about being molested at 6, but recalled the events then. At that point, I was about 19-20 years old thinking that something was wrong with me. What was wrong with me that the same types of events kept happening to me? What am I doing to draw these types of people to me? It was the spirit of perversion. Again, another secret I had to live with, but it still did not stop there. Because I was ignorant at the time, I did not know that this was the spirit of perversion in full operation.

MISADVENTURE

The next school year, my mother allowed me to borrow her car. I noticed the professor following me in his car. He also tried to hit me one time while I was walking across the campus circle. I worked in the science building and cleaned the classrooms at night. My old supervisor from the summer had gotten a residency offer in Philadelphia and relocated. The assistant supervisor took his place. One day he called me in his office and said we needed to talk. He shared with me that my previous supervisor told him what happened to me over the summer and to look out for me. Therefore, he told me that he was concerned. The professor pulled him to the side to let him know that he was concerned about me and my grades. This put my new supervisor on alert. He became concerned about me, himself.

Therefore, again, he let me know that he was there to look out for me and my safety. He let me know he empathized with me. He was really pushing me toward reporting him. He then shared with me how his daughter was violated. Therefore, I begin to wonder how much of his concern was genuinely for me and how much was vengeance for his little girl. I really did not know what to do. I had watched too much Lifetime television and was overwhelmed. After meeting with my supervisor, I was walking to class and one of the minority professors saw me and asked me what was up with me. He had heard my grades were slipping. I replied, "You too?"

I asked him where he had gotten that information. He told me the professor. I began to freak out because not only had this professor tried to hit me while I was driving my car, he also tried to hit me while I was walking across the street. He began to show up in the building at night where I worked. This man was stalking me. Again, what was I to do?

I began to tell the minority professor all of the events which had taken place and the conversation I had with my supervisor. He first apologized on the professor's behalf and told me that I needed to inform the Dean of Students. I really felt this thing unraveling now. He convinced me that I needed to report this and that he would go with me if I needed him to accompany me. Therefore, we walked over to the Dean of Students and met with her. I told her what happened leading up to that particular day. She had the nerve to ask why I brought the minority professor with me to meet with her since he had nothing to do with this. She also said that the other professor had already told her that I was upset because I did not get the grade I thought I deserved.

In actuality, she did not believe me. Immediately, regret took over. I was upset that I had even allowed anyone talk me into speaking out about the incident(s). Therefore, in all fairness, she agreed to at least meet with him and get his side of the story. She said that she would meet back with me only. I told her that I would not meet with her alone. I told her that the minority professor must accompany me.

About a week later I get a call from her office to come in and meet with her. I contacted the professor immediately and asked him to attend the meeting with me. She apologized to me. She said that the professor admitted to everything and that this was his first incident. Then she told me that it was imperative that I went through counseling with the school. Needless to say, I flunked out that semester. I earned 3 F's and a C⁺. I had a .58 Grade Point Average (G.P.A.) that semester.

That Christmas my mom bought me a tape deck for my car and a leather coat. Once she found out that I had been put out of school, she took back both my leather coat and tape deck. I remember her being so angry with me and disappointed in me. I felt like a complete failure. I thought my life was over. All my dreams had ended, so I thought. Little did I know that Jeremiah 29:11 was in effect for my life. God had a plan and an expected end for my life beyond this let down.

I had to write a letter of appeal to be re-admitted for the next semester. I was on pins and needles the entire Christmas break waiting to see if they would accept me back as a student. The truth be told, I really did not want to go back there because of my bad experience. However, I had no other plans for my life. I felt like I had let so many people down that I must return.

God granted me favor and I was able to return the next semester. Unfortunately, my semester G.P.A. was not high enough to bring my cumulative Grade Point Average up to a 2.0. The following year, which would have been my junior year, although my grades continue to improve each semester, I still was not able to bring my cumulative G.P.A. up to a 2.0. I was dismissed from college again. I wrote another letter again for the 4th time. This time they were adamant about my not returning.

I was devastated, hopeless, shamed and had not a clue of what to do with the remainder of my life. I had nowhere to turn and nobody to turn to because I thought I was a failure. I was too ashamed to return home. What would my family, friends and church members think? Too bad my deliverance from the opinions of others came much later in my life. Otherwise, I would not have gone through all of this alone. Regardless, God knows what is best for us. Our footsteps are ordered by Him.

THOUGHTS TO PONDER

- ❖ Some things are not your fault; Some things are (deal with it)
- ❖ Put the blame where it belongs
- ❖ Get delivered from the opinions of other people
- ❖ Recognize and admit when you need help
- ❖ Do not be afraid to speak up; tell the truth
- ❖ You have to walk your process all the way out; there are no shortcuts

NOTES OF INSPIRATION

_____
_____
_____
_____
_____
_____
_____
_____
_____
_____
_____
_____
_____
_____
_____

Chapter 4

HOMELESS AND HOPELESS

While I was in school, I attended a Baptist church under their watch care program. I met a lot of people there. In addition to that, some of my friends from college and I, use to party on the weekends. We met some guys. To make a long story short, we met their families and they loved us. They considered us to be good wholesome, Christian girls. They would often times have us over for dinner on Sundays. I was in the midst of trying to find a place to live in Harrisburg when my car broke down. I had no job, no money and no place to lay my head. My mother encouraged me to come home, but I just could not bring myself to do it. Not that anyone had actually said this to me, but I felt like I could not come home without some type of degree or success.

HOMELESSNESS

I will never forget this day; my car broke down on the side of the road in Harrisburg, Pennsylvania. I was literally stranded. Everything I owned was in the car. I lived out of my car. I would park at a hotel and sleep in my car. Sometimes, I would try to spend a night at people's houses for a night or two. That day my car broke down, I was forced to call my mother. She, in turned, called my Uncle E.C. in Baltimore. He had a garage and towing company. My car and I were towed to his garage. My mother came to pick me up from his garage after she got off work. I refused to tell her that I had no place to go. I was determined to get back in school. I filed an appeal with the college against the decision to dismiss me. They recommended that I go to Community College for 2 semesters and try to improve my Grade Point Average that way, and then reapply for admittance.

Anyway, I had a meeting scheduled with them. That is how I was able to get back to Harrisburg after the car was fixed. Otherwise, my mother would not have allowed me to leave the state of Maryland. I was told that my appeal was rejected. I went to church and some kind of way, one of the members offered me a job at their hair salon as a shampoo girl. I thought this was funny considering I could not do my own hair. That solved the job piece, but I still had no place to lay my head. Eventually, my boss and his wife were influential in finding me a place to live with an elderly woman. I did it as long as I could.

She had a little poodle and you know I do not do animals at all. Not only that, when you walked in the house, it smelled like DOG, Murphy Soap Oil and cigarettes. However, I weighed my options; shelter, car or Fe Fe (the dog)? She had a powder room downstairs, but only one bathroom that we both shared. She was pretty hefty in size and walked with a cane. The bathroom was seniorized, if that is even a word. The toilet had a toilet on top of it and it always had defecation stains on the back of it. Again, I had shelter.

Fortunately, she had a maid that came to clean 2-3 times a week. However, I still refused to sit on the toilet. Do you know how hard it is to go to the bathroom standing up? I will leave the rest to your imagination. Nonetheless, God was still good. Continuing on; the maid smoked and she was okay with it. So on the days she cleaned the house, it smelled like ammonia and a bowling alley (go figure). Well my life then was no different than now. I was always on the go and never home. That became just a place to lay my head.

She began to complain to the people who connected us how I am never home and never spend time with her. Needless to say, I had to find someplace else to live. I guess she took the roommate thing kind of seriously, huh? She just wanted company, God bless her heart. Keep in mind that at this time I was only around 20-21 years of age. I lived in Harrisburg but worked in Carlisle. That was roughly a 35-45 minute ride depending on traffic. She complained that I came in the house too late. If I was not in the house before she went upstairs for bed, she would put the chain on the door. Therefore, I paid rent, but I had to be in the house by 9:00pm. There went the social life. All and all I guess there were some crossed wires in our communication. I thought I was just renting a room. She thought I was there to keep her company all day. If I kept her company, I would not have had to pay rent.

I went to visit some of the family members of the guys we used to date. After much begging and pleading, they allowed me to stay up in their attic. They had turned it into a bedroom for the daughter, but she slept with her mother every night anyway. Thank God for deliverance. During the time I lived with the elderly lady, I still worked at the hairdresser's. I tried to get accepted into other universities, but they would not accept me due to my G.P.A. I eventually ended up going to Harrisburg Area Community College (H.A.C.C.). I had enough transfer credits that I was able to get my Associates degree within a year's time.

At that time, I also had a job working for Hershey. This is when the *Kisses with Almonds* first came out. I thought I was rich. I started out making $11 an hour. That was good money back in 1989-90. I also worked the night shift and was paid night differential. Ooh Wee. Eventually, I was able to secure my own and first 1 bedroom apartment. I thought I was doing it. While attending H.A.C.C., I got my G.P.A. up so I could re-apply to my previous college and was accepted. Once I was accepted back into school, I kept my job because I had lost all of my scholarships and grants when I did not maintain a 2.0 G.P.A. Ooh, if I had known then, what I know now…My my my my my.

HOPELESSNESS

Eventually I moved back on campus living in the dorms again, Praise God! No, for real, Praise God. Anyway, I was able to earn money through the work-study program on campus. Like now, I had two jobs and enrolled in school full-time. All was going well and one day I got a letter from the school saying they understood that I was involved in a sexual assault case with a certain professor and they found out that he had assaulted other women on campus. Their compensation to the victims was a support group and mandatory counseling. I was livid.

Now, all the emotions and feelings were coming back. I became so angry and bitter to the point I literally became ill. After I went to the first support group, I met some of the other young ladies. I was the only minority. I was also the only one that had not actually been raped by this man. I was the only one still, in what I thought, was my right mind. After that, I had an urge to just burn the campus down. Why? If they had just listened to me and done something about that man years prior, none of those girls would have become victims. No, the school was focused on restoration for this professor. I will even go a little further to say that because I was who I was, a minority, if you will, is why nothing had actually been done about my particular incident previously.

I went into a deep depression. I began to blame myself for this because had I only filed a police report, had I only came out with my story, had I only… I was dealing with so many emotions of regret, guilt, shame, anger, suicide, murder. I did not know what to do with myself. Some events transpired and I had to attend J-Court (it was a council set up to deal with in-house situations). My mom and Aunt Carolyn drove up to support me. It was then I was forced to share with my mother everything that had taken place leading up to that point. When she found out I was sexually assaulted, she marched across campus into the president's office and demanded to see him.

His secretary was hemming and hawing. My mother was not hearing it. She walked into his office anyway without being invited. I was frightened for this man. I began to intercede: "Lord, my mom is too old to have to go to jail. Please do not let her go to jail on my account." Unfortunately, the president was adamant about forgiveness and restoration. He did absolutely nothing about the case. We eventually sought legal counsel; however, that is another story for another time.

As requested, I did start meeting with the counselor. It was at that moment I realized that Caucasian and African-American people are different when it comes to expressing emotions and crying. This lady kept telling me I needed to cry. She said I needed to deal with and accept my feelings and emotions. Although she was correct, she harped too much on the needing to cry aspect. Well I guess you could say she finally had a breakthrough with me. Eventually I got mad enough and exploded in her office. Growing up, we were taught to be strong. I was trained by my mother. She would beat me or knock the snot out of me and then say, "I dare you to cry," or "You better not cry either." Really, you just beat the crap out of me and I am not supposed to cry? Yeah, right. Well over time, that is who I became: a person that laughed a lot, but cried little.

What eventually caused my explosion in her office was the fact that I had gone to the support group. Thinking back now, God even had his hand on my life then because I ended up having to be the strength for the other ladies. It was like I had already processed my experience to some degree where I was able to at least pick up and function in life: the Grace of God. This one girl in particular who was in my graduating class missed a few support groups. I asked about her and found out that she was no longer with us because she went crazy. She had to be placed in a mental institution. I was livid about that.

You are talking about a person now having extremely mixed emotions. On one hand I was so grateful that God kept me. I was able to function and Keep Everything Moving. So all I could do was thank and praise Him for sparing me. However, on the other hand, I was angry; not so much because it happened to me, but because it happened to those other ladies and they were not able to handle it. They were for real, basket cases. Over the next twenty years, I learned that I, too, was a basket case and had been affected by this ordeal, but carried mine out differently and a little longer.

I was using denial and because I did, that kept me bound for years. Okay, going back to my explosive counseling session. After I found out what happened to that young lady, I had so much anger and rage bottled up inside of me. I purposed in my heart that I was going to burn the school down. The only thing I was trying to figure out was how to do it without certain people getting hurt because I had a lot of friends on campus that I sincerely love to this day. In blaming the school for some of this, I wanted to pay them back for messing up so many of our lives. Not only that, we also learned that this man's perversion did not stop with women. He molested some boys in his scout troop. All this information came out after my incident. What is ironic is after he left me the day of the sexual assault, he went to meet up with his Boy Scout troop on a camping trip and then on to a family vacation.

Needless to say, I went into the counseling session and went off. I kept seeing visions of the man that had molested me back when I was 6-7 years old. I had nightmares. I felt and saw a dark presence in my room at night. I was scared to go to sleep and scared to stay up. Eventually, I was scared to sleep alone. Me and one of my best friend's at that time, Dee, would spend a night in each other's dorm room. I hung with a group of people and many nights we would hang out in the lounge and just fall asleep there. That was so soothing for me at that time. I told the counselor that I hated the school, I hated myself, I hated the man, I hated everybody. I told her that I was going to burn the school down and that she needed to get her possessions up out of the office. She kept trying to tell me it was not worth it and that I would end up in jail. For some reason at the time, jail did not matter (until I ended up there later in life as you will read in another chapter). All I could think about was paying this school back for what it had taken all of us through. I will not mention the high tuition we paid to go through this experience. Anyway, she gave me her card and told me that whenever I felt that way, to give her a call. I told her, "S-U-R-E."

Girl Gone Wild - I left out of that session, drove to the gas station, purchased a gasoline container and filled it with gas. I purchased cigarette lighters and matches. The first thing I did was set the counselor's card on fire. To this day I do not remember this, but I ran into one of my male friends that I use to hang out with. He said he saw me on my way to my car and he asked how I was doing and what's up. He said that I looked very despondent and I told him that I was fine and I was about to burn the school down. I do not remember it, but it had to be true because before I could pull off from the gas station, he had a group of people and my boyfriend at that time, packed in his car. They did not know what was going on because up to this point, I had not shared anything with anyone. I was too embarrassed that I had allowed this nerdy looking old man to even enter my space.

Some talked to me while others prayed, doing major warfare. They tried to get the gas container from me, but I did not let it go. Different ones said different things to get the gas container from me. Eventually, I gave in because I knew I did not need gas to start a fire. We all went back to campus. God had my friends in place to surround me like a shield. He is a keeper!

Needless to say, I stopped going to the counseling sessions. She kept calling me on the phone and would try to counsel me that way. She was trying to tell me I was sick and needed help. I kind of knew that, but I did not want their help. I knew that I was in a place mentally that only God could bring me back. I went off the deep end. My grades dropped again and they tried to expel me from school again. I was supposed to graduate that year, but did not. I had enough credits to graduate, but my cumulative G.P.A. fell below a 2.0 again. I met with the Dean of Students and they decided that my experience on that campus affected me to the point that I needed a fresh start. They sent me to Temple University campus in Philadelphia.

That move to Philadelphia turned out to be the best. Because I had been in school forever, I did not need any credits, so I got to take any classes I wanted. I was a communication's major and always wanted to be a news broadcaster like Renee Poussaint (Channel 7 On Your Side). She was always in the community helping people.

As mixed up and confused as I was, I always had a heart to serve/ help others. I prophesied my life at the age of 5. I said by the age of 13 I would be a minister, musician and missionary. It's funny how I remember that, but spent years running from the call and assignment on my life. I did not do those things at age 13, but I am an ordained and licensed minister, I used to be Minister of Music at my previous church. I have been a missionary since growing up at First Baptist Church, New Hampshire Ave. and Randolph Streets, N.W. D.C. My motto: **If I can help somebody as I travel along life's way; then my living will not be in vain.**

THOUGHTS TO PONDER

❖ Have friends that are not religious but have a relationship with God
❖ It is okay to cry and it is okay to admit when you are weak
❖ Get the help you need when you need it
❖ Be angry but sin not
❖ Do not allow the sun to go down on your wrath
❖ You cannot run from your assignment
❖ Some yolk only God can destroy

NOTES OF INSPIRATION

_____
_____
_____
_____
_____
_____
_____
_____
_____
_____
_____
_____
_____
_____

Chapter 5

EDUCATION & SEPARATION

Those two semesters at Temple University I made the Dean's list. I was on the other side of the list this time. To God be the glory, great things He has done. After my long six-year journey, I was finally able to graduate May 1992, with my Bachelors of Arts in Communication: life was looking up. I remained in Philadelphia after graduation. I rented a room from one of my professors and landed my first real job with benefits making $19,500 a year. Eventually, I joined an awesome ministry, Freedom Christian Bible Fellowship under the leadership of Pastor Gilbert Coleman Jr. That would turn out to be the next best decision I made with my life. All was well and life was grand.

Upon graduation I entered the field of social work as a case manager for the next two years. The first day on my first job out of college, I was riding with my supervisor to a meeting. This is when the three-car accident I mentioned earlier happened. Needless to say, I spent my first week of the job out on sick leave. July 31, 1994, I lost my job. I was unemployed exactly one year to the date. I started my new job July 31, 1995. I had to solely rely on God. Back then, unemployment only lasted six months. There were no extensions. My six months were up and unemployment had run out. I had a car, an apartment and student loans to budget on no income. At the time, I temped and temped with several different agencies until they had run out of assignments for me. I accumulated a garbage bag full of rejection letters from job applications and interviews. I was either over or under qualified. It got to the point where, at times, I had no bus fare to get to scheduled job interviews.

I found myself depressed again. I stayed in the house for 30 days. I am talking major depression. There was no television or phone; just me, God and an empty refrigerator. I had no choice but to fast (if that is even considered a fast). When times are rough like that, not only do you need a savior, **you need to know that God has a plan for your life.** At that time, I did not know if I would come out, get through, make it or what; but I knew in that particular situation, running home to Mommy was not an option, although she would have loved for me to come home. In the midst of my storm, God gave me a song on April 10, my birthday.

Song of Deliverance - During my 30-day shut-in, somewhere towards the end, a shift took place. **You cannot encounter the presence of God and stay the same for too long.** Every morning I would have devotion in my pink Women's Devotional Bible. This particular morning I had decreed when I got up that no matter what was going on in my life, I was going to enjoy my day. Over time, I learned this should be our response every day. "I will bless the Lord at all times: His praise shall continually be in my mouth (Psalms 34:1). My attitude was 'this is the day that the Lord has made, I will rejoice and be exceedingly glad in it.' I read Psalms 63. God gave me what I called a song of deliverance to bring me out of that stupor. The Scripture read:

> vs.1 O God, thou are my God; Early will I seek thee: My
> soul thirsteth for thee, my flesh longeth for thee in a dry

and thirsty land where no water is; vs.2 to see thy power and thy glory, so as I have seen thee in the sanctuary. vs.3 (The song) [Because thy loving kindness is better than life, my lips shall praise thee. vs.4 Thus will I bless thee while I live; I will lift up my hands in thy name. vs.5 My soul shall be satisfied as with marrow and fatness; and my mouth shall praise thee with joyful lips]. vs.6 When I remembered thee upon my bed and meditated on thee in the night watches- vs.7 because thou has been my help, therefore in the shadow of thy wings will I rejoice. vs.8 My soul followeth hard after thee: thy right hand upholdeth me. vs.9 But those that seek my soul, to destroy it, shall go into the lower parts of the earth. vs.10 they shall fall by the sword: they shall be a portion for foxes. vs.11 But, the king shall rejoice in God; Everyone that sweareth by Him shall glory; but the mouth of them that speak lies shall be stopped.

This scripture was so timely for me because during this time I was going through something with the leaders of the praise team ministry at the church. I was sat down from ministry because my leader accused me of something that was not true and I just snapped on him. I was known for that back in the day. I am much, much, much better now. Look at God….. **Won't He do it?** Anyway, I felt like I could not take anything else at the time. Therefore, this scripture ministered to me and in turn, I ministered it back to God. My song of deliverance came from vs. 3-5 of the New International Version (N.I.V.): 'Because your love is better than life my lips will glorify you. I will praise you as long as I live, and in your name, I will lift of my hands. My soul will be satisfied as with the riches of food. With singing lips, my mouth will I praise you.' I just continued to minister this song unto the Lord until the spirits of oppression and depression broke off of me.

Also, during this time, my pastor, Bishop Coleman and Ms. Deb (his wife), came and just dropped groceries off at my doorstep. They rang the bell and left. Needless to say, with the help of God and the leading of Holy Spirit, I got through that season of my life. Shortly after that meltdown, my Godparents, the Ruleys, came to visit me. They could not believe how I was living. Although I had the cutest little apartment, as soon as you came in the door there was a hallway. My laundry was piled high to the ceiling. I remember Mrs. Ruley saying, "We did not send you to school to get an education to live like this." They were like okay, you need a plan. They strongly suggested I go back to school or something. It just so happened that I had a catalog from Temple University and Cheyney State (the name at that time). We looked at some possible career fields. I had not a clue what I wanted to be or do.

EDUCATION

I always desired to be a teacher but felt like I was not smart enough. I literally hated social studies and science. I did not want to teach pre-school because they were too needy at that age. I did not want to do elementary school either. I did not think that I was creative enough and definitely did not have chalkboard-handwriting. Notwithstanding, I decided to check into a master's' program in teaching. My preference was high school.

The following day, I went to see my friend, Dee. I told her about my decision to look into a master's program for teaching. Her father overheard me and said he was doing the same thing. He actually had an appointment that very same day with an advisor. We went up there together. Because I did not have any coursework in a major subject in terms of my undergraduate degree, I was ineligible for a high school certificate. I would have to go back and take a certain amount of classes before I would be admitted into the program. Therefore, I had to settle for a major in elementary education. Yikes! Even so, it was a foot in the door. Furthermore, because my Grade Point Average (G.P.A.) from undergraduate school was so low, I was accepted on a conditional basis. It was imperative that I maintained a B average. Hallelujah, I graduated with a 4.0 G.P.A. The rest is history.

While I was unemployed, I ran into a young lady from my church named, Vashti. She had not been to church in a good long time. When I ran into her she told me about her job. I congratulated her and told her that I was looking for one. She then commenced to give me the information to the agency where she worked. To make a long story short, I was hired and started within a week. From that point, my life began to look up again. I started school and my new job around the same time, July 1995. I finished my course work in December of 1996. It took me 1-1/2 years to complete the program. However, I did not graduate until May, 1997. Unfortunately, I was only on that job for six months. I was on assignment. I was sent to get Vashti and bring her back to church.

Although I touched many of the young people's lives while I was working there, my assignment was Vashti. We would talk daily. I continued to preach Jesus, battered her about paying her tithes and offering and then some. Before long, she was back at church and involved. I, on the other hand, was out of a job. I lost my job again after six months; somewhere around January, 1996. It seemed as soon as she made the decision to give the Lord another yes, my assignment ended there. I went through hell on that job with the supervisor and the people in that office. I told Vashti that I went through hell for her.

Therefore, she had better stay with God or else I would snatch her up myself. Regardless, it was worth it. It was not about me, but about a soul.

Even though I knew this was the hand of the Lord, I was really feeling like two cents now. I thought to myself, *not another drought Lord. Didn't I get it right the first time?* One thing holds true though: God is not a man that He should lie, nor the son of man that He should repent: Hath He said, and shall He not do it? Or hath He spoken, and shall He not make it good (Numbers 23:19)? **Our footsteps are ordered by the Lord more than we know** (Psalm 37:23).

A lady at my church worked at this Christian school. All of her children went to this school. Initially they all rode the school bus to school. However, when her youngest was of school age, there was some rule or law that he was too young to ride the school's transportation. She and all five of her children at that time would have to ride public transportation across town to get to work and school. Since I was unemployed, I committed to sow a seed in her life until God opened a door of employment for me. I would get up every morning to pick up and drop off her and the children at school. She was pregnant and eventually had to go on maternity leave. I continued to pick up and drop off her children every morning and afternoon faithfully. I did this for about a month.

One day, Dr. Marilyn Miles, the principal/owner of the school, asked me if I was looking for a job. She said she saw my faithfulness to picking up and dropping off the children at school. She said she had a position available in the resource room. To tell the truth, I had no idea what that was or what that meant other than a job. I shared with her how I recently started a Master's of Education program for teaching. I told her I did not know what to do, but I would give it a try. Although I did not officially go into special education as a certified teacher until 2000, that was the beginning of my working with students with special needs.

I literally only made $500 every two weeks. My share of the rent alone was $450. I was faithful and gave God $100 every two weeks: $50 Tithes and $50 offering. You do the math. It was rough because there were still other bills that needed to be paid. I was getting $10 a month in food stamps. Ha, what was I supposed to do with that – go buy a pack of lunchmeat and eat a slice a day? Nevertheless, strangely enough, as I look back over that time period in my life, I did more and had more than when I made more money. God provided. He was true to His promises. He supplied all of my needs.

My friend Dynita and I rented this condominium in West Philadelphia. This place was absolutely beautiful. It had a large indoor pool, social room and then some. Anyway, I took Dynita to a cookout at my play brother Cary's house. She gets pursued by Mark Washington. Within a year's time of our moving in together and attending the barbeque, she got married and moved out. My play sister, Paula, moved into her room. Within a year's time, she got engaged, married and moved out too. So I thought to myself, *clearly, the anointing to get married is in this room.*

I moved to their room. Meanwhile, my friend Lynette moved down from Connecticut. I gave her my old room. The favor of God was on my life. The owner allowed me to stay and pay only my share of the rent until they found somebody else to move in. Initially, Lynette was not working so everything fell on me financially. To make a long story short, about 6-8 months after Paula had moved out, we had to move. I told God, "Okay, two people slept in this room and got married. I move into the room and we have to vacate the premises." The owner found someone that could afford the entire rent.

Something was wrong with that picture. I took it personally. Both Lynette and I had to find somewhere to stay. She went one way, I went the other. I slept here and there until a friend from my church, Rhonda, opened up her home to me. I slept in her den. Thank you Jesus for sending me help from on high. Eventually, I started the job with the School District of Philadelphia. Shortly thereafter I found a house to rent not too far from my job.

SEPARATION

Following this episode one Sunday morning, I was ironing my clothes for church. I got a phone call that my best friend from Messiah College, Dee, had died. She was only 25. I had just spoken with her over the phone that Friday night. It was a Sunday morning. I was floored. She told me how she had been having pain in her big toe. She said the doctors told her it was a pinched nerve. Anyway, I prayed with her that Friday night. She was on my mind all day Saturday. I kept saying I needed to call her.

That Saturday, they rushed her to the hospital because she could not breathe. They found out that she had blood clots. After they got her somewhat stabled her family left to go get her some clothes. While they were gone, the clots traveled to her heart. She went into cardiac arrest and died instantly, just like that—25 years old. I'm like, okay God, Dee? Not Dee Lord. We were extremely close. Absolutely nobody on the face of the earth had anything negative to say about her. She had the voice of an angel, the smile of the bright sunshine and a personality second to none. I could not believe it. I felt like when she died, a piece of me and my hope, trust and faith in Jesus died. It was like, how in the world am I going to make it past this? **But God...........................**

THOUGHTS TO PONDER

❖ Whatever you are facing, it is not the end of your story
❖ Earth has no sorrow that heaven cannot heal
❖ He was there all the time
❖ Be faithful over the little things
❖ Do unto others as you would have them do unto you; not as they do unto you
❖ Love no one to the point you miss/leave God

NOTES OF INSPIRATION

_____

_____

_____

_____

_____

_____

_____

_____

_____

_____

_____

_____

_____

_____

Chapter 6

MICE AND MEN

Eventually, I was trying to purchase a home and decided to go the *lease with option to purchase* route. I rented the house and rented rooms to two of my good friends from college: Lynette and Patrice. Of course I moved in the house, but had no furniture. I cannot remember what had happen at that time, but for some reason, I had no bed. Some nights I would sleep on a pallet in my room, other nights I would sleep on the couch. The man I was renting from left the couch and the dining room table. I had injured my leg over the Christmas holidays when I came home and I was on crutches.

MICE

I did not like the carpet in the room so I pulled it up little by little. One night I was lying on the floor and a mouse ran across my foot, I hollered and crawled to the door of my bedroom. I was trying to get up off the floor. I dragged myself across the floor. My foot rubbed across the nails that were in the floor and ripped a piece of skin off my foot. I am hollering and crying because you have to know one thing about me; I do not do animals, critters, creatures, bugs or any of the above. How God called me to the mission field is beyond me. Anyway, I scurried on my elbows in an attempt to drag myself out of the room. My roommate, Patrice, yells up from the bottom of the stairs, "Boo (my nickname at the time), are you alright?"

I begin to yell back down to her, by this time I had made it to the hallway, "No, I'm not alright. Don't you hear me screaming?" Meanwhile, Trice didn't budge from the bottom of the stairs. She was not coming up those stairs for anything. After getting myself up off the floor using the banister in the hallway, I finally told her about the mouse. Eventually I hopped my way downstairs on one leg to the couch. That ended my days of sleeping on the floor. That also led to one of my biggest mistakes ever.

MEN

Mistake is defined as 1) To understand (something or someone) incorrectly; 2) To make a wrong judgment about something; and 3) To identify (someone or something) incorrectly. I misjudged someone and understood their role in my life incorrectly. As a result, an unfortunate incident occurred in my life. I was doing social work for an agency and met some new friends in Philadelphia. I was a tomboy growing up and always had close male, platonic friendships. As a matter of fact, I was the 'Best Man' in my best friend, David Brook's wedding. However, to be politically correct, in the program they listed me as Best Friend and I stood at his side during the ceremony. Even after my negative experiences with men, I was still able to maintain a healthy perspective about men and realize that all men are not dogs and perverts.

I befriended this one guy from Africa. We became really close and use to hang out. I often went over to his house and he would show me lots of videos and movies from Africa. That is when I understood why we, as a people, cut up at funerals. We brought that straight across the waters. I saw it with my own eyes. Anyway, he had a 1 bedroom apartment. His nephew wanted to come over to the United States for school. He sponsored his nephew to come over. He upgraded from a 1 bedroom to a 2 bedroom apartment. His nephew came to live with him. Within about three months' time, his nephew met a nurse. They fell in love. He moved in with her and eventually they got married. That left my friend with an extra bedroom.

From time to time, I would spend a night over there. He gave me a key. I would call to let him know when I was coming. The good news was that he worked nights so he was never there when I was. I never stayed there if he was off on the weekends. My then pastor's sister-in-law, Ms. Pat warned me not to stay over there. Of course, being who I am, gullible at times, I was like, oh no it's alright. He is cool peoples. Besides, he had a girlfriend. I met her and we got along very well. As a matter of fact, we all use to hang out together.

Well I was leaving for the Bahamas to take the youth to a *Youth Alive* Conference at Miles Monroe's church. He knew that I was going out of town and was giving me what he called some pocket change. This was two days before we were supposed to leave. I called to tell him that I was staying at his house that night. He told me to call when I was headed that way. I did not think anything of it. I arrived at his house, showered and went to bed. Mind you, he had to work that night. He stopped at the house on his way to work. I was already in the bed sleep when he came home. He came in the room and woke me up. He said that he was just dropping the money off. I told him to put it on the coffee table on his way out for work.

Initially he was talking to me from the doorway. Then, he came and set on the edge of the bed. Still, I thought nothing of it. He leaned over and tried to kiss me. I pushed him away and was joking like, "Man, what are you doing? You know your girlfriend does not play that." I brushed it off. I turned towards the window and told him he better get out of there and get to work before he was later than he already was. Then I asked him to turn the lights out on his way out of the room. I had no idea what I was in for that night.

To this day, I do not know what all happened, but he tried to pull the covers off me. I told him to stop playing. He left the room. I thought all was well. When he came back into the room he did not turn the lights back on but he walked over to my bed. Next thing I know he was trying to pull the covers off me again and pulling on my panties. Needless to say, I was raped that night. I fought and yelled and screamed and squirmed as much as I could. I scratched his back and face up pretty badly to the point I had skin under my nails. But that did not stop him. While he was raping me, he pinned my arms down to keep me from swinging and fighting him any longer. All I remember is that I was extremely dry inside. Every stroke felt like someone had broken a Coca-Cola bottle and was just ramming it into me. After about 20 minutes, I stopped fighting and thought if I lay there it will all be over soon.

He finished doing what he had to do, jumped in the shower and went to work. I just lay there in tears. I just knew that I was cursed because I kept allowing the same types of incidents to happen to me. Then I thought I had something wrong with me because maybe I was drawing this type of attention/activity to me. I lay there for a while after he left trying to figure out what to do. My clothes were ripped, the bed was all messed up and blood was all over me and the sheets.

When I discovered that I was bleeding, I immediately got up and jumped into the shower. I scrubbed and scrubbed and scrubbed my body trying to wash the entire event away. My skin had turned red and I was close to rubbing my skin off. I was scared to touch my private area initially because it was just throbbing. Although the incident was over, I still felt like he was inside of me. My pelvic area was hurting and sore. All of a sudden I wanted my mother.

I just fell down in the shower while the water was running. Water was beating me all in my face. I wanted to die. I did not think that I could face the world any longer and say I allowed myself to be mishandled/mistreated again. This time, there was no liking to it. I really do not know how long I sat balled up in the shower. I just remember the water getting cold. Eventually I got out and went into the living room. I was shivering. I could not bear to walk in that room again. As a matter of fact, when I finally did leave his house, I left with the clothes on my back. I left everything else that was in the room there because I did not want to go back in there again.

I tried to call my mother, but I kept hanging up. I was scared. I thought she was going to get on me for even staying at his house. I called 911 and hung up a few times. Eventually they called back and asked if everything was okay. That scared me to death. I finally called Ms. Pat from my church and told her what had happened. She told me to call the police and to get out of there. Although she was one of the ones who told me not to stay over there, not once did she say, "I told you so." However, I felt her saying it in my spirit. She used to tell me, I was a single young lady. He is a single young man and I do not want people to see me come out of this man's house. It did not look good. She always said, "Do not let your good be evil spoken of." I was like, ah, you just do not understand. I am tired of sleeping on the floor, the couch is uncomfortable and every now and then, I just like sleeping in a bed. The bed in his guest room was so comfortable too.

I told her that I could not call the police because I was staying in this man's house. How would that look? Then, all I began to think about was the fact that in two days I was leaving to go to the Bahamas. I really was in no position physically, mentally or spiritually to go anywhere with anybody, let alone be responsible for somebody else's child. No way. I had just made a huge mistake with my own life. I did not want to be held accountable for anyone else's. However, I could not cancel because the church had paid for my flight and it was a non-transferrable ticket. I had a pretty good relationship with both my pastor and his wife, but I was scared to tell them. Because I was already blaming myself, I could not handle anyone else pointing their finger at me too. Hence, I got myself together, put on my game face and went to the Bahamas.

While in the Bahamas, I had to share a room with two of the young ladies. We decided that we would rotate sharing the bed. The first night I had a bed to myself, while the other two young ladies shared a bed. That night I had one of those dreams where you have to go to the bathroom and you go to the bathroom in your dream, but in your dream you still feel like you have to go. Lo and behold, that last time I went to the bathroom in my dream, I started going in real life. I woke up and caught myself. Then I ran to the bathroom. By the time I got to the bathroom, there was only a trickle left. I cleaned myself up and was really embarrassed then. I was, like, I cannot believe that I am almost thirty years old and wet the bed. Really?

I placed a glass of water on the nightstand. When everyone woke up, I purposely spilled the glass of water to make it look like that is how the bed got wet. I told everyone not to sit on the bed. There were two other female youth workers on the trip with us. They shared a room with some of the other young ladies that went on the trip as well. That morning, I sent the other girls over to my room and told the other youth workers about my wetting the bed. I was so scared that something was really wrong with me.

I felt I was on the verge of having a nervous breakdown. I did not want it to happen on that trip; mainly because I was a youth leader. Many of the young people looked up to me. The way I ended up telling them is I played off wetting the bed. We laughed and joked until I laughed and cried. Then they saw that my tears were for real. I just broke down and told them everything that happened with the rape. I kept blaming myself and they were trying to reassure me that it was not my fault. I did not believe them, however.

That night we got together with the young ladies and we ended up having girl talk. The way things went, the Holy Spirit had me share my experience with the girls in the sense of telling them to be careful and to watch the positions they put themselves in with men. Of course, No, means no, but all men do not understand that. We had some major breakthroughs with all the young ladies from the youth group that evening. Although I was not happy about my experience as painful as it was, mentally and physically, **I came to grips that night with the fact that if I had to go through that so that others might be free, healed or escape that experience, then it was worth it; just as long as God got the Glory out of it.** At that very instance, God changed my mishap and mistake into a message. K.E.M. (Keep Everything Moving).

THOUGHTS TO PONDER

❖ Even if you think you have the right away, do not put yourself in harm's way

❖ One's Man's misery is another man's mission

❖ You can either rehearse it and nurse it; or curse it and reverse it

❖ If you play in the mud expect to get dirty

❖ Listen to wisdom (sound advice)

❖ Welcome constructive criticism

❖ Slow down when approaching a brick wall

NOTES OF INSPIRATION

_____

_____

_____

_____

_____

_____

_____

_____

_____

_____

_____

_____

Chapter 7

PAIN AND PURPOSE

Send Me Lord: I'll Go

Back in the Mid 90s a song came out, *Where He Leads Me I Will Follow*. The words were as follows:

> Where He leads me I will follow. Where He leads me I
> will follow. Where He leads me I, I will follow my Lord.
> I'll Go with Him all the way. On a mountain high, or in
> a valley low; I'll go-o-oh...I'll go with Him all the way...
> Send me Lord I'll go ooh; I'll go ooh ooh, I'll go ooh,
> ooh, ooh. I'll go with Him all the way!

At my previous church in Philadelphia, Freedom Christian Bible Fellowship, we use to rock that song. We would get all excited about that song, especially on the, "I'll go ooh ooh" part. It never failed, Bishop Gilbert Coleman Jr., my pastor at that time, would come behind the choir, exhort the congregation into a high praise, and then break up the praise party by asking if we really knew what we were singing. He would ask if we really knew what the words to that song meant?

He went on to explain that when we sang that song, we were saying, "Yes, Lord. Yes, I'll go wherever you lead me." Then he would ask, "What if God told you to go to Africa, to China and other parts of the world?" In my mind, I would snicker and think God knew me. Therefore, He knew not to ever require something like that from me. Bishop Coleman began to talk about the different customs around the world. For example, he asked, "What if God sent you to China and when you sat down to eat, they placed dog in front of you?" He explained you would have to eat it in order to be polite. I was like, nah, not me. Of course, some of the hallelujahs died out.

However, over all, the congregation would praise God the more. Some yelled out, "Yes, yes Lord." At times, my pastor would lead us into the Church of God in Christ's (C.O.G.I.C.) version of Yes: "Yes, yes, yes, yes, yes, yes." Some people would begin to moan and cry out to God saying, "Yes." We would end up in worship. Some people would be at the altar or on their knees at their seats. Others had hands lifted while tears streamed down their faces. Nonetheless, even then, I too questioned how many people, including myself, really meant that we would go in a valley low or was it just a nice song to bump and move to. After all, it had a nice beat.

Personally, I knew I would never go to China or Africa. I hated being teased about being so dark when I was growing up. I made it a point to omit phrases of songs that I did not agree with. I did not want to sing what I considered a lie. I would pick back up on the words or the verse of the song that I agreed with or believed to be true. I know; crazy right? I still do that to this day.

Nevertheless, I would sing that particular song at the top of my lungs. In my heart of hearts I really believed I would go, I would do, I would obey. I would be silent on the "where He leads me, I will follow" part and pick back up on "I'll go with Him all the way." I know, it makes absolutely no sense. They both mean the same thing. Go figure.

Unfortunately, I had no idea of the magnitude of that statement. I did not estimate the highs and lows; hills and valleys. Most of the time, we think of blessings, peace, joys, happiness, prosperity and wealth being God's will for our lives. We or shall I say, I, did not realize or take to heart that **sometimes brokenness comes before blessings; poverty before prosperity; passivity before peace; jail before joy and humiliation before happiness.**

Prophecy - My journey started with a word spoken into my life in the middle of a Sunday morning message on June 21, 1998, more than 15 years ago. I remember it as if it were yesterday. It was youth Sunday on a Father's Day. Bishop Coleman preached a sermon entitled, *Be A Man*. In the middle of the message, he called out my name and prophesied the following to me:

> It's been rough here. You've gone through because the place where God is taking you is in distress. You've gone through what they're going through. You weathered the storm, but you're going through the eye of the storm. The people will be going through, but you will not be moved. They will wonder why you're standing and how you can make it through when all hell is breaking out. You have to get ready to move. It won't be a sudden move, but start looking in 1999. In 1999 begin to look and it won't be a move back home either.

Bishop Coleman went back to his message as if there was nothing to it. Now that song, *Send Me Lord, I'll go ooh ooh* took on another meaning in my life. I began to understand why my life moved to another dimension. I understood why I begin to feel empty inside. Previously, I had been seeking God and asking Him, "Is this it or is there more to life?"

I felt like I was at the end of my rope until I heard that prophecy. That was the answer to my question(s). The reason I felt that way, was that my time in Philadelphia was dwindling down. As a result, God was making me ready so I could begin to detach myself mentally, physically and emotionally. Philadelphia had become my home away from home. I had some real hard times, but I loved it. I would not trade any of my experiences for anything in the world. Philadelphia embraced me and welcomed me with open arms. My church family became my family. I blended in really well with the people and the culture in the city of brotherly love.

To conclude this section, one day as I walked in downtown Philadelphia before I relocated to Chicago, I ran smack dab into my rapist. I had not seen or heard from him since that night. He spoke to me as if nothing ever happened. He reached out to embrace me. I put my arm out to stop him. I looked at him dead in his eyes and said, "I forgive you," and kept on walking. I felt such a release in my spirit after that. I knew that the power of God was working in my life. The old Kem would have punched him dead in his face and then spit in his eye. But God... What the enemy intended for my harm, God turned around for my good so that many lives would be saved (Genesis 50:20). Thus, that is why you are reading this book today.

God turned my pressure into praise and my pain into purpose. **I am who I am today as a result of all I have encountered, experienced and exited (left behind).** I know that as you read this book, you will notice that at times I insert humor into some serious situations. Regardless of what I have been through and how I perceived my overall life experiences, I bless God. He gave me a sense of humor.

True, at times I laughed to hide the pain; but when you see me laughing now, it is because I won. Satan was/is defeated, Hallelujah. I can **Laugh Out Loud at the enemy** because he is a defeated foe. **God kept me so that I would not let go**.

PAIN

We all have experienced deep-seated pain in our lives before, whether physical, emotional, spiritual or psychological. Pain is Pain. The good news about pain is that it is an indicator that something is wrong. In essence, our pain has a purpose. Just like our physical pain is an indicator in that something is wrong physically; emotional or psychological pain is an indicator that something is wrong spiritually. What I have gone through in my life was extremely painful to me and for me. What made it even more painful is that I had to go through it alone. Well, I did not have to, but I chose to do so. That caused lots of pain, which brought on some illnesses in my body.

For many of us, our mental disposition caused some of our pains. There are numerous studies out there that link cancer, arthritis, high blood pressure, diabetes not just to our bloodline and eating habits, but to regret, unforgiveness, bitterness, anger, and offense, etc... In reality, **holding on to things we should let go of can cause sickness in our bodies, which in turn, leads to pain.** Fortunately in my case, my pain led to my purpose. I am called to minister to wounded people: saved and unsaved alike. I have a passion for hurting people and God has graced me with compassion to push people through painful situations in their lives. This next section is about getting to the root cause of your pain(s).

Pain Killers - Painkillers are superficial just like whatever we choose to use to deal with our problems. Because one chooses to drink, smoke, snort cocaine or overeat to ease the pain, it is only a temporary fix. Painkillers do just that, kill the pain, but not cure the cause. Just as natural diseases call for natural cures, spiritual diseases call for spiritual cures. Food may ease the pain, but after that bucket of chicken has been digested, symptoms of loneliness, bitterness, anger, low self-esteem, rejection, rebellion etc...return. I am a witness!

Painkillers are deceivers. The enemy will allow you to continue to use them to mask the underlying pain. If he can get you to think/ believe that you are better, that you are healed or cured, then you will not seek God for the underlying truth. That is what happened to me. Food became my lover. Another way to look at it is, when the doctor prescribes antibiotics he tells you to complete the entire bottle even if you begin to feel better. Because many of us began to feel better, we stop taking the medicine and the symptoms return within weeks. We then have the nerve to claim we do not know why we cannot get rid of this bug. **You cannot partially treat it; you have to treat it fully.** You have to take all of the medicine. True, it may be a hard pill to swallow, but it is the process to your healing.

In the Bible, Asa, King of Judah, was diseased in the natural because he was sickened in his spirit by anger. What caused his anger? His rejection of the truth. He did not want to receive the truth about his actions (II Chronicles 16). He did not want to take responsibilities for his actions, just like many of us. We blame others or the devil for the mistakes we made. Flip Wilson use to say, "The devil made me do it" (I am dating myself again with that one). By the way, I use to have a Flip Wilson doll. Moving right along, it is not the devil that causes us to sin and make carnal decisions. Rather, it is when we are drawn away by our own lust (evil desires) and enticed (James 1:14).

The Bible also states that For all that *is* in the world, the lust of the flesh, and the lust of the eyes, and the pride of life, is not of the Father, but is of the world (1 John 2:16). When we do what we want to do and then refuse to accept the truth about our action, we deceive ourselves. Asa became so angry it affected him and those around him. Other people's action can affect us, just like our actions can affect other people. This is how you get a Spiritually Transmitted Disease (STD). "Whoever heeds instructions is on the path to life, but he who rejects reproof, leads others astray" (Proverbs 10:17). Physicians may kill the pain, but only Jesus can truly heal the pain and the root causes of it.

When one catches a cold, it has to run its course. There is no natural cure for the common cold unless we rebuke the spirit of infirmity. We will pop pills and drink cold medicine to cope with the symptoms of the cold, but at the end of the day, we still may have a cough, fever, runny nose and perhaps a sneeze here or there. No longer can we rely on man-made remedies for spiritual weaknesses and sicknesses. We must look to God. "All of our help comes from the Lord," (Psalms 121) not the world. Doctors practice medicine by saying try this remedy/prescription and follow-up with me in a few weeks. That is why it is called a practice. However, you do not need a follow-up check up with God. He is omniscient. He knows and sees everything. "Certainly the LORD watches the whole earth carefully and is ready to strengthen those who are devoted to him..." (2 Chronicles 16:9 NET).

We must turn our hearts to God so that He can turn His strength towards us and heal us of all our STD's. "If my people, who are called by my name humble themselves and pray and seek my face and turn from their wicked ways; then will I hear from heaven, and will forgive their sins, and heal their land" (2 Chronicles 7:14). There is a remedy for sickness; Tylenol, Aleve, Motrin or Morphine are not it.

2 Chronicles 7:14 lets us know what we need to do individually and collectively to be healed.

We must first humble ourselves. Yes, you got yourself in the mess you are in. You may have even made a mess out of your life. People may have wronged you and you feel you have a right to be angry, but, humble yourself before the Lord. He, not your friends, family, pastor(s) or yourself for that matter, but God Himself, will lift you up out of that dreadful place (James 4:10). When you humble yourself under the mighty hand of God, at the proper time He will exalt you (1 Peter 5:6). **Humble yourself enough that you do not want anything before its time and season.**

When you turn your heart towards God and humble yourself, He hears you when you pray. "Then He said unto me, fear not, Daniel (Kemberly, put your name here): For from the first day you set your heart to understand and humbled yourself before your God, your words have been heard, and I have come because of your words" (Daniel 10:12). In this instance it took 21 days for Daniel to hear back from God because of principality and rulers of darkness in high places; nonetheless, God heard Daniel from day one, just as He will hear you and me when we are willing to admit our weaknesses, mistakes, frailties and know that without God, we are nothing. When we humble ourselves, that puts us in position to receive His grace: "But He gives more grace...God opposes (resisteth) the proud, but giveth grace to the humble (James 4:6). **Being humble also calls us to repentance. This is basically us telling God that He was right and we were wrong.** God, we missed the mark. "If we confess our sins, He is faithful and just to forgive us our sins and to cleanse us from all unrighteousness" (STD's), I John 1:9.

Pray. Simply put, communicate with God. Many people believe that prayer is just one-way in terms of us talking to God; however, it is a two-way process. Prayer is a beseeching of the Lord (Ezekiel 32:11); a drawing near to God (Psalms 73:28). In essence, it is communication with God, listening and talking with Him. Prayer develops our relationship with God. As we communicate with God, we grow more intimately connected with Him. Think about a relationship between spouses, friends or family members. To learn of one another, there must be some form of communication between a minimum of two people not just a talking back and forth. There must be effective communication. According to Merriam Webster, communication is the exchange of information; a message. It is a process by which information is exchanged between individuals through a common system of symbols, signs or behavior.

Another way to look at communication is a two-way process of reaching mutual understanding in which participants not only exchange (encode – decode) information, news, ideas and feelings, but also create and share meaning. It is a means of connecting people and places (Business Dictionary). According to dictionary. reference.com, communication can be defined as something imparted, interchanged or transmitted. Sounds like prayer to me. There are four purposes of communication: to inform, ask, persuade or entertain.

Regardless of the problem, prayer is the solution. Prayer is the conduit through which all the power and provision of God flows (Apostle Jennings). When we pray, we are not to pray the problem, rather pray the solution, the answer, if you will. As we pray, we are to allow the Holy Spirit to pray through us; pray in faith; pray the word; and pray boldly with confidence.

Seek His Face – According to Merriam Webster, seek means: a) to resort to; go to; b) to go in search of; look for; c) to try to discover; d) to ask for; request; seek advice; e) to try to acquire or gain; aim at; f) to make an attempt; try; g) chase; pursue. The following is an example of seeking the Lord:

(Daniel 9:1-27) In the first year of Darius the son of Ahasuerus, by descent a Mede, who was made king over the realm of the Chaldeans—in the first year of his reign, I, Daniel, perceived in the books the number of years that, according to the word of the Lord to Jeremiah the prophet, must pass before the end of the desolations of Jerusalem, namely, seventy years. **Then I turned my face to the Lord God, seeking him by prayer and pleas for mercy with fasting and sackcloth and ashes.** I prayed to the Lord my God and made confession, saying, "O Lord, the great and awesome God, who keeps covenant and steadfast love with those who love him and keep his commandments, we have sinned and done wrong and acted wickedly and rebelled, turning aside from your commandments and rules…"

Turn from your wicked ways. It is hard to seek His face and not turn from our wicked ways. To put this plain and simple, stop doing wrong. Stop acting immorally. If you are doing something that goes against the word of God, it is merely wrong. If you are uncertain if there be any wicked ways in you, seek the Lord. Believe you me, He will reveal and deal with them. However, you must be open. Do not allow the spirit of pride to creep in and tell you, "I am all right or okay." We all miss the mark at times. "For all have sinned and fallen short of the glory of God" (Romans 3:23). If you want to know what is ailing you or the body of Christ, remain humble, pray without ceasing, seek the Lord's face and turn. **Do not park in your mess. Turn from it (about face).**

PURPOSE

I have a message to every female, young and old alike: regardless of what you have been through, regardless of the mistakes you may have made; no one, and I mean no one, has the right to violate you. I went through a leadership development class at my church and I learned that we are not our experiences. True, our experiences help make us the persons we are today; but my testimony is like that of David, **"It was good that I was afflicted..."** (Psalms 119:71). What I do know is that it does not matter whose fault it was: yours or somebody else's. What is important is God allowed it and should get the glory out of it. My birth certificate was a death certificate.

The enemy has been after my assignment since I was in my mother's womb. He knew that my mother carried greatness down in her belly. He knew I was a mover and a shaker. He knew that I would affect nations. Therefore, he wanted to silence me at a young age from the beginning. I spent years in depression being what is known as bipolar and schizophrenic in the spirit. I was up one day, down the next. Happy for one day, depressed for one month. I went from "God is good all the time" to "my God, my God, why hast though forsaken me?" **But I can declare to you this day that I am free. I am free to love, not just others, but myself.** I hated myself for years because of what I had been through, but I had to learn that **we all must go through a process.** Guess what? **Your process is tailor-made and handpicked just for you.** What the enemy intended for my harm, God turned around for my good so that many lives would be saved (Genesis 50:20).

God was not stingy with me. I am a very gifted, talented and creative person. I can pretty much do anything that I put my mind to. However, this Attention Deficit Disorder (ADD) keeps me from focusing on any one thing too long (like completing this book). Honestly, I started writing this book 14 years ago. However, from the time I signed a contract with my publisher, until now, literally took 9 months… Distractions. I am musically inclined. I have played several instruments throughout my lifetime. I tried the drums, but that definitely was not my purpose here on earth. I played sports: basketball, volleyball and softball. By the way, I was a tomboy growing up and I loved playing football, especially in the snow. I ran track in high school and college. I sang and wrote music, poems, plays and books. I have the gift of exhortation. I am prophetic and called to preach God's word. I am an evangelist, missionary and teacher. I am a motivational speaker.

You may be wondering why I shared all that. The reason is, **God put too much in me for me to just allow the devil to stop me in my tracks over bad experiences and decisions, pain and problems.** I am greater than what I have been through. **I am more than the sum total of my experiences. As a matter of fact, I am a greater person because of what I went through.** I have an assignment to spread the gospel around this world and I cannot do it effectively all jacked up in my spirit. I had to walk out my process and deal with Kem. Then, I allowed God to heal me. I had to face myself and recognize that I was operating in the spirits of rejection, rebellion, anger, bitterness, unforgiveness and all their cousins, as you will read in a later chapter. I have a purpose for being on this planet and so do you. We have a place called destiny to get to and the enemy would love for us to stay focused on the trivial things of life so that we do not walk out our

God given assignments. **God put a deposit in each of us. He will cash in on His investments.**

Even after discovering your purpose and/or assignment(s), I would be misleading you to make you think that all will be hunky-dory. However, what I can let you know is when you submit to God and allow Him to be the captain of your ship, you may hit some rough waters and high waves, but the impact of the stormy winds and waves will be lessened through God's grace. **Do not be like me and focus so much on your pain that you miss your purpose.** You have a rendezvous with destiny. Keep Everything Moving (K.E.M.) and get there!

THOUGHTS TO PONDER

- ❖ You can experience peace when your life is in pieces
- ❖ Remaining stuck is a choice like moving forward is a decision
- ❖ Pain is an indicator that weakness exists
- ❖ Problems come before and with purpose
- ❖ Pain is a part of the process; Relax and trust the process

NOTES OF INSPIRATION

_____

_____

_____

_____

_____

_____

_____

_____

_____

_____

_____

_____

_____

_____

_____

_____

Chapter 8

OBEDIENCE AND OPPOSITION

God began to put things in motion for my transition to Chicago, Illinois. I happened to tell a co-worker that I was relocating there and she knew a priest that was on the board with this principal. She contacted him and I sent him my resume. He, in turn, forwarded it to the principal in Chicago. I spoke with her and we set up for me to fly out for an interview. The priest wanted to interview me as well to work at a summer camp he ran every year. The favor of God was in motion.

OBEDIENCE

Although I did not know a soul in Chicago, I was obedient to the voice of the Lord. I trusted Him to work everything out. One of my friends at church, Sonja, had a best friend in Chicago named Beddar. She contacted Beddar and told her that I was moving out there soon. Beddar, in turn, contacted her sister-in-law, Leslie, and told her about me. Her sister-in-law contacted me. She offered to host me for the weekend of my interview. What a mighty God we serve. When I arrived in Chicago for the interviews, the priest picked me up from the airport. He took me to see his church and interviewed me for the summer camp position. I was hired. We then went to one of his parishioner's houses on the south side of Chicago. He spoke to her about me. She offered me a room in her house while I got myself situated in Chicago. I was extremely apprehensive based on my last experience staying with an elderly person, but had decided to stay with her for at least the summer while I worked at the camp.

From there I went on my interview at the school. I was hired on the spot. At some point, we met up with Leslie and she showed me around the area of Chicago where I would be working and may want to live. We went apartment shopping. I found an apartment that I really liked at South Commons and I put in an application. Unfortunately, my cycle came on the night before I left to return to Philadelphia. I was ill for the next several days.

When I returned to Philadelphia, I made an appointment with my gynecologist. She ended up scheduling me for surgery. I was unable to take the job for the summer. The priest was upset with me. He thought that I turned the job down because it did not pay that much. I tried to explain to him that I had to have a procedure done, but I still do not think he believed me. I contacted the lady that I was supposed to stay with and explained to her the situation as well. She understood, I guess, but was disappointed. She said that she was looking forward to having me stay with her. She also stated that she liked my personality and thought we would get along great. Meanwhile, I prepared for surgery.

As with all of my surgeries, my mom came in town to be there with me. The doctor did a procedure: laparoscopy/hysteroscopy in which they go in and scope you. They were trying to rule out endometriosis. It turned out that I had polyps. That is what caused the excruciating pain while visiting Chicago. Although it was a simple procedure, recovery was horrible for me. Nonetheless, I eventually bounced back. I spent the remainder of the summer healing and preparing to move.

I ended up staying with my friend Quinnette (Mi Mi) before relocating to Chicago. It did not make sense to have to find an apartment for that short period of time. Meanwhile, the apartment complex had contacted me to let me know everything looked great, they were just waiting to hear back from one of my landlords. I used the remainder of the time to go through all of my stuff and get rid of some junk so that I would not transport any unnecessary items to Chicago. Unfortunately, some of my things were damaged due to mildew in one of my other friend's garage.

A woman named Geraldine from my church was from Chicago. She was moving her niece or nephew down from Chicago at the time. She told me that her brother and nephew could help move me to Chicago. She agreed to pay for half of the rental van. I would use the van going up, and they would use the van coming back. We rented a seat-less fifteen-passenger van. Look at God. He was setting me up for a smooth transition, so I thought. We agreed that we would ride up overnight. My mom and my friend Kristy caught the train to Philadelphia to also help with the move. My friend, Rodney, also came along to help with driving.

Opposition

Right before I got ready to take my nap at 3pm the night we were supposed to leave, the rental office from South Commons Apartments contacted me. The rental agent told me, "Ma'am I meant to call you back to let you know that you were not approved because we still had not heard from one of your previous landlords." I could not believe it.

I said, "Ma'am, we are leaving tonight to come to Chicago and you are telling me when I get there, I do not have a place to live?" She said they would keep trying. I asked her what time they opened. I told her we would be there in the morning. I hung up the phone and, of course, cried. Yet at the same time, I said, "God, I need you to handle this. You told me to go to Chicago and I am following your command. At this point I am walking out of total, obedience, trust and faith." I had nothing else left.

I went to meet my mother and Kristy at the train station that evening. When I saw my mother I just leaned on her and started crying. I told her about the apartment. She asked me what I was going to do. I told her God said to move to Chicago. She told me not to worry about it and that God spoke to her the night before to tell her to pray. She told me everything would be alright. Praise God that she was obedient. While driving my car, mom fell asleep at the wheel. When she woke up, she was about to run into the rental van. He kept us!

What is ironic about all of this is you know when you tell people that God told you to do something; they look at you as if you are crazy. Well my mom, this time, did not really offer any opposition. She knew that I did not want to move more than two hours away from home, and certainly was not looking forward to a wind chill factor that went below zero degrees. However, the night before we were supposed to go, my mom said that God spoke to her in an audible voice. She said that it was like roaring thunder. She said she heard him say, "PRAY"! My mom said at the time she had no idea what to pray about, but she got out of her bed and got her knees to pray. She said she prayed and told God that it was in His hands, whatever it was.

South Commons - We arrived in Chicago. It was still early in the morning. The rental office was still closed. We decided to have breakfast and hang out in a restaurant until they opened. Meanwhile, everybody was praying in his or her spirit. We got to the rental agent's office and she did a lot of going back and forth with the manager's office. Of course, I was in tears, but at the same time, I had peace. I really wanted that apartment to work out because I was comfortable with it, it was close to my job and Leslie did not live to far from there. We waited and we waited. Finally the lady came out to tell us that I got the apartment. She even said to me, "God loves you because they do not do this for anybody." My address was 2605 Indiana Ave, Apt. 1009. I was on the 10th floor and had a view of the lake and the south side of Chicago. It was absolutely beautiful.

My mother and friends stayed with me for a few days. We went up to the school where I would be teaching to see my classroom and to try to get it together. In Chicago, they use the term grammar school and it started at pre-kindergarten, if it had a state head-start program. Otherwise, it ran from kindergarten to eighth grade. I was scheduled to teach the eighth grade class. When we walked in the room, the previous teacher was moving his things out of the room. He was upset because he liked that room. We walked in and saw a bullet hole in the outer layer of the window. We had a view of the projects right across the street. We asked him what was up with the window. He explained that the Gangster Disciples (GDs) and the Blood Disciples (BDs) got into a war and one of the bullets hit the window. Why did he say that in front of my mother? That shot her blood pressure straight up to the roof. Of course, the question became: are you sure God said Chicago, or are you sure He said this school? I had a lump in my throat as well. However, I assured her this was God's will for my life.

We went to the teacher store to purchase supplies for the room. We set the classroom up. That Sunday we went to New Covenant Missionary Baptist Church, Dr. Stephen J. Thurston's church. His brother, Stanley Thurston, was the Minister of Music at my home church in Washington, D. C. My mother was good friends with his sister, Charlotte, who had lived in D.C. for some time. However, she had moved back home to Chicago. We went to their house and had dinner with the family after service. The Thurston family was quite warm and welcoming to me. All of a sudden, Chicago was not looking so large to me. I believe I ended up dropping my mother and Kristy off at the airport somewhere between Monday and Tuesday.

After they left, I went to the grocery store to begin to buy a few things for the house. I spent all of my money moving and so I did not have much money left. My mother left me with a few dollars. I came out of the grocery store, put my groceries in the car and the car would not start. I told Misty, my car, to stop playing. I did not know what to do. Some guys were hanging around and they came to check on the car when they saw my hood up. Each of them had their opinion about what was wrong, but none of them could get the car started. I thanked them and sent them off. Then I sat in that car and prayed. I said, "Lord, at your word, I packed my stuff up and moved. I barely know anyone here, what am I going to do? Father I need you right now."

I put the key in the ignition, turned it and the car started. I had intentions of going to a few other stores, but I drove straight home. I did not pass go and I did not collect $200. I drove directly home. I called Bishop Coleman. I was upset because I saw my faith beginning to waiver. I told him how I did not understand how this could be God's will for my life with all the opposition. I thought that when you obeyed God that everything would work out smoothly with no bumps in the road. I will never forget what he spoke to my spirit that day. It was my first true lesson on The Will of God. He said to me, "Kem, because you do what God told you to do, that does not mean you put your guard down. Even when the children of Israel got into the promise land, they had to fight." For whatever reason, that was a revelation for me.

I no longer bellyached over my misfortunate circumstance. Instead, I thanked God for keeping me in the midst of it. Then he turned around and told me that they had to rush Ms. Deb, his wife, to the emergency room. She ended up having a panic or some type of anxiety attack when I left. She and Bishop Coleman knew that I was moving to Chicago on Faith. Bishop knew all was well. Ms. Deb, I believe, feared for me. I was like a daughter to her so she had concerns.

School started and all was well. I met some new teachers and everybody was really nice and friendly to me. I hated when people asked me what brought me to Chicago. Naturally, my response was, "God." I could read some people's minds: weirdo. Truthfully, I had no other response. Who in their right mind would pick up and go somewhere where your tears literally froze up in your tear duct. They did not even get a chance to stream down your face. Not only that, but the wind was strong enough to just push your car into another lane.

Howling Winds - I will never forget this. It was a few nights after everyone had left. Mind you, I was living on the tenth floor. The way this apartment was set up, the balcony was outside of my bedroom, but the door to access it was in the living room. As I slept, I heard this noise. I did not know what it was, but it sounded like somebody was out there. I cannot even find the letters to type to even make the sound. I was scared. I called my mother around 3-4 o'clock in the morning. I said, "Mom, I think somebody is on my balcony." She was half asleep, half annoyed and half scared because I called her at that God forsaken hour in the morning.

She said, "Kemberly, what do you mean that somebody is on your balcony? Don't you live on the 10th floor? How can somebody be out there? Well why in the world are you calling me? Call the police."

I said, "I do not know, but they are out there. I hear them. They keep banging up against my window. They are making these noises and I described what the noise sounded like: whoooooooohooooohooooo." By the time I finished, my mother was hot with me.

She said, "Girl, get off of my phone. That's the wind."

I was dumbfounded. I had never heard the wind like that before. I knew in nursery school they taught us that March came in like a lion and went out like a lamb. They even went as far as to say that the wind howled. However, that had never been my experience. She told me to get off her phone and we hung up. There was something deep down inside of me that was still scared though. I refused to go and check the noise out to see if my mother was correct or not. However, my solace was the fact that whatever was out there had not made it inside my apartment yet. Such goes my introduction to Chicago, Illinois: the Windy City!

THOUGHTS TO PONDER

❖ God makes provision for the vision
❖ Your foot steps are ordered by the Lord; Just make a move
❖ When it is time to go, it is time to go
❖ Opposition does not necessarily mean you missed God
❖ Embrace change
❖ Walk by Faith and not by sight
❖ Do not take it lying down; stand up and fight
❖ Test(s) precedes a testimony

NOTES OF INSPIRATION

_____
_____
_____
_____
_____
_____
_____
_____
_____
_____
_____
_____
_____

Chapter 9

PRISON, PAUL AND SILAS

At work, I met a young woman by the name of Lesa. We hit it off very well. I really liked her because we both spelled our names with an E as oppose to an I. She sounded the most enthused about her church when I asked different teachers what church they attended. They were having something that night and I went to visit. My assistant principal, Mrs. Vera Curry-James (at that time), also invited me to her church. For about a month or two, I bounced between the two churches. I would go to Sunday school at Emmanuel Baptist and go to the morning service at Prayer and Faith Outreach Ministries under the leadership of the then, Pastor William Hudson III. Since then, he has been elevated to the office of Bishop.

Eventually I joined Prayer and Faith Outreach Ministries because at the time, it reminded me of Freedom. It was hard to join any church initially because I had so much of Freedom Christian Bible Fellowship inside me. I was looking for another Bishop Gilbert Coleman Jr., but the Holy Spirit reminded me that there was only one Bishop Coleman and only one Freedom. I had to release that experience in my spirit and embrace the new. It was prophetic that

God sent me to Chicago. There I got a fresh new wind in the Windy City. Disappointingly, my misfortunes followed me to Chicago.

In August 2000, I went on a trip with Pastor Hudson to Pilgrim Cathedral of Atlanta, Georgia. Bishop Kent and Diane Branch were the pastors. This began the succession of knee injuries. While on the trip, we were horsing around in the hotel. It was Marcus and Michael Maloney, Yetha Parks and I. Michael had thrown water on Yetha, but got my hair wet. We made a point to get Michael and Marcus back. To make a long story short, Marcus had an ice bucket filled with water and tried to throw it on me. I tried to kick the bucket out of his hands. He in turned grabbed my foot. I tried to kick him and twisted my leg. The bucket fell and he ran down the stairs. I felt something in my knee pop.

We were in front of Pastor Hudson's room door when all of this happened. I could not get off the floor. I crawled to his door to let them know I was hurt. He thought we were still playing and told me to call Jesus. Then he said it serves us right for playing around. Yetha helped me get back downstairs. My knee was swollen and I could barely walk. The next day was our last day there and we had already decided to go sightseeing. I was the designated van driver for this trip. I tried to tell Pastor Hudson about my knee but he did not want to hear it. He told me to get in that van and drive. Of all the places to tour, we went to visit the Kings' family church and home. This just so happened to be a walking tour. I was in so much pain, but I had to K.E.M.

We left for the airport that evening. I ended up getting a wheelchair once we arrived. My pastor thought I was faking. I tried to show him my knee, but he did not want to see it. My friend Lesa picked me up from the airport that night. I had her take me straight to the hospital. The hospital was literally right across the street from my apartment building. I told her I would just catch a cab home. By the time I got to the hospital, my entire leg was swollen. The X-rays showed that there were no broken bones, but to follow up with an orthopedic doctor. They wrapped my leg, put it in one of those immobilizers and gave me a pair of crutches.

Any given day, it would take less than five minutes for me to walk from home to the hospital. I thought I could just walk home since it was right across the street. That was one of the longest walking journeys ever. It took me nearly 30 minutes to get from the hospital home. Why I did not call the cab is still beyond me till this day. The next morning my friend Lesa came and picked me up for church. We still had our tent up from the tent revival. When I hopped in there on those crutches, Pastor Hudson was so shocked. He kept apologizing saying he thought we were playing. He still stuck to his guns by saying serves us right; a bunch of grown folk running around throwing water on each other in a hotel.

Eventually, I had to have an MRI, which showed a torn meniscus in my right knee. This would be the first of four surgeries on that same knee. I had the surgery a day or two before Thanksgiving. My mother and nephew, Eddie, came up for the surgery. I was walking without the crutches within about three days. I was off from work for several weeks though. When I went back to work, I had a little altercation with my principal.

I do not remember the ends and outs of how and why everything happened the way it did, but for some reason she told me I had to leave the school. I did not understand why she could try to put me out; I worked there. Some of my possessions were in Lesa's room. I was headed to her room to get my things so that I could leave. The principal continued to follow me around the hallway cursing and carrying on. I continued to walk and ignore her. When I got to Lesa's room, the principal jumped in front of the door and told me I was not getting anything over her dead body. Again, she told me to leave the building. I told her that I was not leaving without my stuff. I attempted to walk past her to go into the room. This lady reached out and grabbed me by the neck and pushed me backwards. I twisted my knee. I believe I was only four weeks out of surgery at that time.

At that point, I dropped everything in my hands, put my fists up and said, "I had a dream that I was going to have to kick your butt." I pulled my hand back to swing and punch her in the face. However, Holy Spirit just knocked me back. We all looked like what just happened? Once I got knocked back, that is when the assistant principal got in between us. She told me to just leave the building because the principal was out of control. I said, "No, I am calling the police and my attorney first." The assistant principal walked me into the office and I called my attorney, then I called the police. Meanwhile, the principal went into her office to call the police as well.

Do you know when they arrived; they took me out of the school? I was like really? This woman put her hands on me and you are putting me out of the school? So I told them that I needed my paperwork I accidently left in the office. They went and got it and took me outside to get my statement. Well they refused to actually take my statement. Instead, they said that it would be an addendum. They explained to me that she was the principal of the school and I was considered trespassing. I explained to them that I worked there and I do not know what happened. I came to school that morning and she walked into my classroom and asked me to get my things and leave. I never got to the bottom of why she asked me to leave that morning.

The police officer explained to me that by her being the principal of the school, it was like it was her house and if she wanted me off the property I had to leave. Still today, I do not understand that considering I was still an employee and had not been fired or anything. They took me to the police station and I attempted to file a police report. Unfortunately, they would not allow me to file charges. I was not able to make my own report, however my report had to be an addendum to the principal's. I was furious. In my mind I thought, this woman does not know I will burn that school down with her in it.

The school district gave me a few days of leave with pay while they tried to find another school to transfer me to that semester. Meanwhile, I reinjured my knee that I just had surgery on the month prior. The doctor ended up taking me out on workman's comp for several months. However, they refused to pay for the needed surgery of the new tear. We eventually had a hearing. The principal was friends with hearing officer so they ruled in her favor. She lied and said she never put her hands on me. I had a tape recorder of her following me around the school, cursing me out and threatening me. Unfortunately, the hearing officer refused to listen to it.

I continued to fight my workman's comp claim. Eventually, over a year later, they approved the surgery. By then I had all kinds of issues and injuries concerning the knee. One night about a week before the surgery, I had a dream. In the dream, God told me that what they think they are going to find, they won't; that he was healing me. When my mother flew up for the surgery, I told her what God told me in my dream. During the surgery, I was in twilight sleep and I thought I heard the doctor say something to that effect. Once I came to in the recovery room, my mother told me that the doctors told her that what they thought they went in for was okay, but that they had to do a different procedure. Prophecy was fulfilled.

When I came to, my entire leg was wrapped from my ankle to my hip. They had an immobilizer on the leg. The doctor told me that he did an arthroscopic chondroplasty. He said that I would be non-weight bearing for 6 weeks. That meant crutches. The first thought

that came to my mind was how was I going to get up those two
flights of stairs at my apartment. The next thought was how I was
going to lift 2XX lbs. up on the two little pieces of wood. My soul
looks back and wonders how I got over.

MCKENZIE GOES TO JAIL

It was Memorial Day weekend and my mother's choir was visiting
from Washington, D.C. I hung out with her and the choir members
for the weekend. On Sunday, I took them to The Water Tower. While
there it began to pour down rain. We decided to go back to the hotel
for dinner. This particular weekend, my knee was bothering me and I
was wearing a knee brace. After dinner, I left the hotel. I got to my car
and realized that I did not have my cell phone. I double-parked and
went back into the hotel's restaurant to look for it. It was not there.
I went to the front desk; they told me to call security on the lobby
phone. I followed their instructions.

I learned that a phone had been turned in to them. I went to park
the car first. I came back and went to security. I told them the type
of phone I lost. They had my phone. However, the officer at the desk
would not give it to me because I did not have photo identification on
me. I explained the entire day to him. I told him how my mother was
staying in the hotel, how my leg was aching and swollen, etc... Finally,
he agreed to let me have the phone if I could tell him the first three
names in my contact list. I said, Alcourt, A.A. and somebody else. The
man told me no I was wrong. I went on tell him that Alcourt's number
began with a (301) area code, A.A.'s number began with (215), etc.....

This man refused to give me my phone because A.A.'s name
came before Alcourt's. Really? How many people have an A.A. or
an Alcourt in their phone contacts? Clearly, I was working against a

spirit. Not only that, but this man was of African descent. I will say no more about that. He was extremely dark and stood at least six feet tall. There were two other officers in the room and I turned to them to say we had an agreement, clearly, this is my phone. Being a McKenzie/ Worthington, I went around the corner of the desk to the door where another officer was sitting. I asked if he could come out and help me. He said he would be out in a minute.

Meanwhile, the original officer and I were still having words. I asked to use the phone so that I could call my mother so that she could call somebody. I reached down over the counter to use the phone and this man grabbed me. Why in the world did that man put his hands on me? Well, I tell you every negative incident that I had ever encountered with a man, rose up in me, and the fact that my father never put his hands on me. Actually he beat me once. It was a few taps and I had the nerve to say, "It didn't hurt." I am sorry, Dad. Yes, I was crazy. As my mother puts it: stubborn and hardheaded.

In any case, when that man put his hands on me, I reached and jumped up over the counter to try to bust him in the head with his telephone. I also reached over and took my phone. I got put out of the office. I called the police and I called my mother and told her to get down stairs immediately. She called Donna and told her to pray and I believe they both came down. Meanwhile the police officers showed up. The security officers took them into the room and showed them a clip of me jumping across the counter. Not once did they mention that the six foot black man put his hands on me first.

They took me into a room and I was snapping and going off. They kept telling me to calm down. I told them to calm down. I asked how they would like it if some man put his hands on them. I saw the look in my mother's eyes that night as they put the handcuffs on me to escort me out of the building. I felt so ashamed. Again, here is a time when I called the police and I am the one going out in handcuffs. I was charged with trespassing, aggregated assault and battery. What? I could not believe it. I kept asking them to watch the entire tape, but they would not do it for whatever reason. They said that since I was not a guest of the hotel, I was trespassing and the security officers wanted to press charges.

That night McKenzie went to jail. When we got to the jailhouse, a young female Caucasian police officer kept telling me that I needed to calm down. I asked her how she would like it if some big black tall man put his hands on her, she called the police, and she was arrested. Yes, I have a mouth now and had one back then. Before going to jail, I gave my mother my car keys to move the car because I could only be there for a short period of time. I gave her Bishop Hudson, my pastor at the time, Elder Bernice Smith and Minister Ivy Douglas' phone numbers and told her to call them. They were schedule to fly back to Washington, D.C. the following morning and I had not a clue of what would happen to me.

I can say looking back in retrospect that I had a Paul and Silas experience somewhat. They put me in a holding cell. Mind you, my jeans were still wet from being caught in the rain earlier. They took my shoestrings and belt. They took one hand and handcuffed me to a rail behind me. I had to sit on a cold cemented, I do not know what to call it. My cycle was on and there was absolutely nothing I could do. My leg got even bigger because I did not have my knee brace on. I was the only person in the holding room. I sat there for the next hour plus moaning and crying, "Ummmm, uuummmmmmm, ummmmm." At one point, a female officer in booking said, "Ma'am, you are going to have to shut the F - - - up."

I cried louder and harder and had a nerve to say, "How would you like it if you called the police because some big black man put his hands on you and they arrest you?" She told me that was not her problem, it was mine and that I would still have to shut the F--- up. I began to moan, "My God, My God, why have thou forsaken me?"

Eventually, they took my mug shot, ran my fingerprints and put me in a literal jail cell. I could not believe it. I begin to think of all the dumb and stupid things I did as a child/teenager, and now I am an adult and I got arrested off of some bull. Oh, I had a major a-t-t-i-t-u-d-e with God. I felt like He was in control and He could have stopped this. I blamed Him for everything. I had several random thoughts of how I served Him from a little girl to then, how I was sold out for the Kingdom, for real, and this is where it got me. I was like, "Oh, no, I cannot do this anymore. From here on out, I am going to live my life the way I please," (whatever that was; all I knew was God). I was thinking of all the time, financial, and other sacrifices I made to "Live for Jesus," but at the time, I did not feel like Jesus was living for me.

PAUL & SILAS EXPERIENCE

When I made it to the jail cell, I was cold. Again, my cycle was on and I really needed to handle that. I had to go to the bathroom, but in that cell was the same concrete ledge like in the holding room. They also had a toilet and no toilet paper. All I could think was if I even attempted to go to the bathroom, it would be a mess in the making. I had to hold my pee and hold my peace. On the way to the jail cell, the same lady who told me to shut up, asked me if I wanted something to eat. I said, "No thank you, ma'am." Who could eat at a time like that? Not only that, but in jail they really do give you bread and water. She had lunchmeat and bread. There were not even any condiments. Oh my.

When I sat down on the ledge, I was shivering, but at the same time, I became really sleepy. All of a sudden, I felt this overwhelming peace come over me and I could feel the prayers of my mother going forth on my behalf. Tears of joy and gratefulness are streaming down my face even as I type this. Although I was extremely angry with God and the world at that moment, I felt God. I felt His presence with me. At that very instance, I knew and understood what it was like to feel God for real in the face of adversity. I do not know how to explain it, but the words on the pages of the Bible became real and life for me at that very instance. David walked in the room Psalms 27: The Lord is my light and my salvation...; For in the time of trouble He shall hide me in His pavilion...; Wait on the Lord, be of good courage and He shall strengthen thy heart: wait I say on the Lord...; Psalms 139: O Lord, thou hast searched me, and known me. Thou knowest my downsitting and mine uprising, thou understandest my thought afar off. Though compassest my path and my lying down, and art acquainted with all my ways...; Wither shall I go from thy spirit or wither shall I go from thy presence...; If I make my bed in heaven or in hell, He is there.

It was like I thought that something had to happen for me to know that God came through for me, but His coming through was not taking me out of jail at the moment. He changed my emotions and spirit while in the midst of it. I felt Him and knew intercession was taking place on my behalf. I do not know, but I hope you get and understand what I am trying to say. If you have never been in a situation where you felt alone, cold, abandon, embarrassed, ashamed, stupid, including shaking your fist at someone, or as we used to say giving them your butt to kiss after they had done everything for you... If you have never been there, then you will never know the feeling of being comforted, rescued, or delivered. God met me in the jail cell. **If I never had that experience, I would not have had an experience.**

Sometimes we wait for God to deliver us from or out of a situation. He wants to deliver us in the situation. The same was with Jesus and the Jews. They were waiting for Jesus to come and wreak havoc because of the prophecy: "For unto us a child is born, unto us a son is given: and the government shall be upon his shoulder" (Isaiah 9:6). They thought that Jesus would come and fight for them and tear down the other kingdoms. Rather, He came with deliverance, healing the sick and raising the dead. They did not understand Him and could not receive Him or His ministry.

I was going through like the Pharisees and Sadducees. When I called the police, I expected God to show up and show out. I did not expect to have to go to jail. The devil had already lied to me and told me my life was cursed, I was cursed and then he allows a string of lifetime events to take place in my life that were unfavorable to me. Instead of getting pissed off at the devil, I turned my anger towards God. I felt He could have prevented it. Nonetheless, **even in my anger and frustration towards Him and life, He kept and comforted me.** He ministered to me. He loved me. He put His arms around me and literally rocked me to sleep. I fell in such a deep sleep that when they told me that I was being released, I thought it was morning. Well in essence it was the wee hours of the morning. That is the kind of God we serve. He is there all the time!

They told my mother where they were taking me and she drove my car to the police station and stayed there all night. God allowed my mother to find favor with the officer in the front lobby. She explained to him what happened. She told him my testimony about being a teacher, serving in the church and so forth. Technically, because it was a holiday weekend (Memorial Day), I should have stayed in jail from Sunday to Tuesday at the least, But God. I was let out on my own recognizance and the fact that I was a teacher. That was the first time I learned that I could lose my teaching license because I was arrested.

From there, I hired an attorney. After that, we were supposed to sue the hotel and the police department. That never happened. I was never Mirandized when I was arrested. Before we appeared in court, they reduced the charges to aggravated assault and battery. When we went to court, the judge threw the case out of court. He asked the officer if he was actually afraid of me. He alluded to the fact that the officer towered over me. Furthermore, there were three more officers present in the room that night. He also had the other officers in the room come up and asked if they were present when this happened. They told him yes. The judge asked how many people were in the room when the alleged assault took place. The point he was trying to make was that there were more of them than me and this man stood over six feet tall. Certainly he could not have felt threaten: 1) since he put his hands on me first and I responded and 2) there were others in the room. He dismissed the charges, but after watching the video, told me that I needed to work on my temper and anger. That was so true.

After I left court, although I won the case, I realized that I had lost in life. I tell you I was raging mad and literally saw red the night of the incident. I understood that I had been living my life out of anger and bitterness. I would always look for an occasion to snap. I was angry because of all the negativity I had experienced in my life from childhood to then. The enemy began to put my life on rewind and show me all of the bad things that had taken place. He conveniently left out all of the blessings I had encountered throughout my life (deception). I especially could care less about men at the time in my life even though my best friends were men. I hated being black. I hated myself. What was scary about all of this is I was slowly coming to a point where I hated going to church (perception).

In weeks to come, instead of focusing on how good God was, I focused on the devil's lie: how bad my life had been. I know some of you reading this book have been there: so focused on the bad, that you cannot see the positiveness of a situation. When hurting, it is hard to see how good God had actually been to you throughout your life. All you see is event after event, episode after episode. Like me all you see is that you are in jail, but you do not see Him holding you and keeping you in the midst of it. You do not see that your actions put you in the situation. I could have lost my mind for real. He could have allowed my anger to go to the point where I resisted arrest and then some. But God loved me enough and favored me enough to allow me to have these experiences so that I would know Him for myself. I do not have to read about the stories of the characters of the Bible, I lived my own. However, do not stop reading your Bible.

I went through all of this so that I can be a walking, living, breathing testimony of the Goodness and Mercies of God. It really did not matter who was at fault; the enemy, others or me. **At the end of the day, I survived. I woke up to another day to get it right.** Unfortunately, the devil did not want me to see my glass as half-full, rather half-empty. As I continued to go to church, I thought about how long I had been in church. It appeared as if nothing changed in my life. I still struggled financially after all I sowed and gave. I still believed God for healing in my body. I felt like I sat up in church and died. I blamed the church for my issues. The things of God were no longer dear to me.

Growing up, at times when my mother punished me, she hit me where it hurt. One time because of my attitude and sassiness with her, she punished me from going to church on Easter Sunday. I was livid. I loved going to church and she knew it. I was at church just about every day of the week even if nothing was happening. I would go and volunteer in the office. I would clean up the church. I literally just hung out at the church. When I was seven, I asked for one of the big Bibles that the pastors used to sit on the pulpit. My mom purchased it for my birthday. That was the best birthday present ever to me. I loved God and I loved church.

I used to love the things of God; but I came to a point in my life where going to church became a chore. Serving in the house of the Lord was a chore. I forgot the fact that I went to jail and God met and released me. I did not see the fact that my serving in the kingdom kept and protected me. I forgot about the fact that God gave me health and strength to go to a good paying job with benefits every day. All I could see was that 'Nobody knows the trouble I see.'

It actually would not be until I relocated to Atlanta and connected with The Harvest Tabernacle Church under the leadership of Apostle Travis C. and Pastor Stephanie Jennings that I began to understand my life. I was just jacked up by then and did not know it. I knew that I dealt with the spirit of rejection, but I did not know the degree of the hold it had on me. Rejection had sisters and cousins: rebellion, anger, jealousy, bitterness and low self-esteem to name a few.

While in Chicago, I left Prayer and Faith Outreach Ministries in search of God. I met with my pastor and told him it was time for me to leave. We were about to have Sunday morning worship services in a school around the corner from the church. I told my pastor that I was not supposed to go with them in that next move. Although he knew I was crazy, being the loving, caring compassionate pastor he was, he did not want to see me just out there without a covering. He even prophesied to me before I left. One thing he mentioned was that I was going to keep running and eventually run into myself. He did not lie. That is what took place here in Atlanta. He also told me that he had been praying for me and that I should try Pastor John Hannah's church, New Life Covenant. At the point in my life, I was sick of church and church people, especially the black church and how some black churches operated. I went a few Sundays, but I was not ready for them yet. I ended up going to a Caucasian church for a little spell: Rob Thompson. I did not join, but I did attend their new members' class to see if this was where the Lord was leading me.

During that season, I also attended Apostle H. Daniel Wilson's ministry for a while too. I actually went down to join and was stopped in the middle of the isle by an usher. After that, I was just church hopping trying to find a place where my spirit would rest. One Sunday I ended up back at John Hannah's church and finally joined. I ran into my friend Damon. He actually graduated from New Member's class that particular Sunday. The fact that I knew somebody that had come from the same church I attended in Philadelphia made me feel comfortable about this ministry. I began to grow in leaps and bounds in my spirit within that year. I worshipped there until I relocated to Atlanta, Georgia.

I flew to Atlanta for a job fair that was hosted by Gwinnett County Public Schools. Dr. Angela Pringle hired me on the spot. I stayed in Atlanta for the weekend and went to church with my Godfather. One of his frat brothers started a church and it was their inaugural service. The message was 'What If.' It talked about what if Noah had a 'what if?' At that point, I knew that I could not have any what if's in my spirit. I knew then I had to make the transition to Atlanta whether my house sold or not. I flew back to Chicago and put my house on the market for sale. I earned my third master's degree by then, December 2005 and was graduating in May 2006. I threw myself a congratulations/farewell party and moved to Atlanta on Saturday, July 15, 2006.

THOUGHTS TO PONDER

❖ If we could see the unseen dangers God kept us from

❖ Do not allow the devil's deception cause you to miss your blessing

❖ Do not make permanent decisions on temporary trials

❖ Think on things that are true, honest, just, pure, lovely and are of a good report...

❖ Learn to admit when you are at fault; face the consequences and K.E.M.

❖ Learn to celebrate the moments that are painful, that allows God to Be God in your life

❖ Celebrate how far you have come and understand you have far to go

NOTES OF INSPIRATION

_____

_____

_____

_____

_____

_____

_____

_____

_____

Chapter 10

TRAVEL AND TRANSITION

TRAVEL

I was supposed to leave early Saturday morning headed for Atlanta. For some reason, I dragged my feet that morning. My girlfriend, Lesa, allowed me to store the stuff that would not fit in my car in her garage. I got an oil change and got on the road around 1-2 pm that afternoon. Somebody should have told me about the hills of Georgia. It became extremely dark as I drove down through the mountains. There were only two lanes: the opposing traffic and mine. On the opposing traffic side were trees. On my side of the road was only a cliff. I just kept repeating, "Yea though I drive through the valley of the shadow of death, I will fear no evil."

Hot Lanta - I finally arrived safely at the Ruleys. I was supposed to reside with them during this time of transition. Consequently, my Godfather's parents moved down the month prior. My God brother, Jarun, moved back home as well. They arranged for me to stay with the daughter of friends of the family. I was nervous because I had not met her nor seen her house. Praise God that when we arrived, all was well. Rasheeda was very warm, friendly and kind. She truly opened her heart and home to me with extreme sincerity. I was like, Wow, God hooked me up with someone like myself. Anybody that knows me knows that I would give you the shirt off my back even if you did not need it.

I stayed with her for a few months. Although she was not rushing me to leave, I was used to living on my own by then. I had roommates throughout the majority of my 20s and just felt like I was too old to stay in someone else's house even if everything was smooth sailing. I also begin to house shop at the same time. However, I was still not certain as to what part of Georgia I wanted to make my permanent resident. Unfortunately, I moved out prematurely and had to move back in temporarily until I closed on my house.

When I moved out, I had moved to Timber Ridge apartments. They had 2 bedroom lofts. For some reason, I have this fascination with lofts. I currently reside in one. When I went to sign the lease, I did not receive my keys until afterwards. When I moved in, the apartment was not properly restored. The apartment was a mess. To my disadvantage, I already had everything in motion to move. I stayed at Rasheeda's that night. The next day I went over to clean. Ants and roaches were all over the place. I totally freaked out and had a meltdown. I am not talking about little roaches. I am talking about HUGE, big, FAT cock/water/flying type roaches. This was something I had never seen outside of television. I went over to management and complained. Needless to say, I scrounged up the money and got my possession out of there within a day or so.

Of course, they tried to sue me because I broke the lease. On the contrary, they broke the lease by not adequately preparing the apartment. Furthermore, I was not allowed a walk through. I took pictures and videotaped the ants marching around one by one, hurrah, hurrah. My Godfather, Mr. Ruley, and I met with them. To make a long story short, my belongings were in storage. I was back at Rasheeda's. Nevertheless, God was faithful. I closed on my house in the same subdivision as Rasheeda within sixty days.

TRANSITION

I was finally settled in Georgia. It was time to get serious about finding a church home. I visited different ministries based on recommendations, but had not settled on one in particular. I would go to an eight o'clock service at one church and an eleven o'clock service at another. I finally narrowed it down to three churches. I met a young lady named Jawanda at a "Special Education New Teacher's Training." She kept telling me about her church. She told me they were having their inaugural service in October. I brushed her off for a while. One of the reason's I was not interested was because service started late, like at noon or something. I told her she was crazy. Who goes to church that late on a Sunday for a first service? God, Himself has already left the building. The other reason I was not interested was because it was newly established. I wanted a place I could hide in the back, pay my tithe and offering and go home. Yeah right; **to whom much is given, much is required.**

I visited the church. It was okay. There were just a handful of people there, but there was much love among them. They were like a close-knit family. The name of the church was Love Fellowship Tabernacle. The pastor, Aaron Q. Morrison, was out of Hezekiah Walker's churches in New York and Pennsylvania. At the time, the pastor still worked in New York but came home to Georgia on the weekends. They had yet to start having bible study. I attended a few Sundays in a row. During the announcements, they stated they were starting bi-weekly Bible study on Saturdays. In my mind, since I was still trying not to be caught up in doing the church thing anymore, I asked if you needed to be a member to attend. They welcomed me with opened arms. They also stated that they were trying to start a praise and worship team. They were looking for musicians.

What was ironic about all of this is, I had not joined the church yet, but saw the need of the ministry. I told them that I had an eighty-eight key electric piano they could use if they needed it. They were like great; bring it to rehearsal on Saturday. Little did I know that this was a setup from them and God. In their mind, they were thinking, if she has a piano, she could play. In my mind I was thinking, here is a group of faithful people trying to carry out the man of God's vision. The least I could do is offer my substance. I went to the first Bible study. Afterwards we had rehearsal.

It was so cute. We had committed young children playing instruments, rendering their services and hearts to God. I want to say they were either in elementary school or in their first year of middle school at the time. One young girl played the flute while another played the viola. We had other young men who could play the drums. One of which could somewhat play the keyboard. So there we had it. Our band consisted of all children under the age of 17, I believe. Their hearts were so tender. I was blessed as I watched them serve.

Since I brought the keyboard, they thought I would play it. I was like, "No, sir, I do not have gifts like that. I read music." I sucked at playing by ear. I took piano lessons from first through twelfth grades and private lessons in college and as an adult; but no way was I going to try to get in front of people to play. I would sing a solo first. What is also ironic about all of this is I knew how to play several different instruments; but I would not play the piano publicly.

Here I am to Worship - To make a long story short, I became the minister of music. Before you knew it, I was teaching parts, holding musicians rehearsal and playing on Sunday mornings. What in the world was God doing? My pastor's wife was over worship. She would tell us the songs she wanted to sing and we would learn how to play them. We perfected, William Murphy's, "Let the Glory of the Lord Rise Among Us", "Alleluia", and "Here I am to Worship". The latter song was the first song I played with them.

Once again, my 'no' to God turned into a 'Yes.' I told God I was there to worship, not my will but His be done. That Sunday, God anointed us to play that song considering it was our first time ministering. When I saw what having a group of tenderhearted people willing to do whatever and make whatever sacrifices necessary, to usher in the presence of God and serve the man of God's vision, who was totally walking by faith, blessed my socks off. All I could do was worship God.

I always desired to play for a church, but never thought I could do it because at the time, I only read music. In the African-American Gospel Music industry, it is imperative you know how to play by ear. I could pick out the melody; meaning, playing one note at a time, but chords? No sir. During that season in my life, God would wake me up in the middle of the night and the Holy Spirit would give me chords for certain songs. I was not a pro, but God began to use me in that area, in terms of the music ministry. I began to take music lesson from my friend and recording artist, Gregory Wright. I would go on YouTube and learn runs so that I could play shouting music. I must say, God did his thing during that time. Eventually, I was even able to follow my pastor as he preached. Again, **God does not call the qualified, He qualifies the called.** God can take your little and turn it into much if you let Him. Eventually, our services and music went to another level. I felt like we were living out the days of Acts when they were all of one accord, sharing all their substance (Act 2:44-47).

Death knocking at my door - Next thing I knew, I moved up on the devil's hit list. My birth certificate was already my death certificate, but the fire was hot and the flames were high. At the time, I could not understand why. But now it is so clear. When I say a string of mishaps took place, they were not light afflictions. The devil literally came after my very life. He tried to take me out twice within the same week. I went over to the Ruleys' house to hang out. Although I had my own house, I would go over their house every day and stay until the wee hours of the morning.

At any rate, going back to how I could have died. My pop pop and I were in the house. I was working on my PhD at the time so I worked on homework. He watched television. We sat in the house for some hours. The Ruleys came home. As soon as Mom walked in the house she asked what that smell was. Pop pop and I looked at each other like what smell? She asked Pop pop if he was cooking. She was like, "Oh my goodness, is the gas or something on?" He told her, no. Mom finally made it into the kitchen and one of the burners was on, but the pilot was not lit. They were tripping at the fact that we did not smell anything. So in the back of my mind, I was thinking, no the devil did not try to snuff us out of here, but I was kind of joking in a sense.

The next day, Tuesday, January 20, 2009, was our 44th president Barrack Obama's Inauguration. I got in late from my parents' house and slept downstairs on the futon. I had the fireplace going. The Holy Spirit woke me up and told me to get to the keyboard. He gave me a song. The keyboard was near the fireplace. The fireplace was not on any longer. However, I did have it on when I went to sleep that previous night. I forgot about it since it was not on when I woke up that morning. All of a sudden, I heard a hissing sound. It came from the fireplace. I was scared. I prayed, "Lord, I know it's not any snakes in my fireplace." I called my neighbor, Heidi, and told her what was going on. She asked if there was a fire in the fireplace. I told her no. She said it was not snakes, "Silly, your fire went out. That is the gas. Hurry up and turned the pilot off."

I did what she told me. I walked outside of the house and came back in to see if I could smell gas. Sure enough, the house reeked of gas. I open the doors, windows and garage to air the place out. That is when I knew: OMG, the devil really was trying to kill me. Seriously, what were the odds in that type of situation happening twice to one person within two days? But God in His Mercy, had plans and purpose for my life, saw fit for me to live. He blocked it. It was like God would allow things to happen in my life so that I would be able to say, "Oh, no, His word is true." No weapon formed against me shall prosper… however, God's Word will go out and accomplish what He sent it out to do, and it will not return to Him void (Isaiah 55:11). God was and still is watching His Word to perform it over our lives, despite what we think or believe (Jeremiah 1:12).

Okay, in March of 2007, I was injured on the job. I had my third knee surgery in June. The doctor that performed that surgery did not do a great job. In February 2009, I underwent what was called a cleanup procedure. I had my fourth surgery on the same knee, February 19, 2009. After surgery, I was non-weight bearing again. During this time, I was out on worker's compensation. One of my neighbors that I used to work with was in between jobs. I asked her if she would get me back and forth to my therapy appointments. My cousin, Pam, was getting married this particular weekend. I was scheduled to fly out on Thursday, March 19 to attend the wedding; crutches and all, so I thought.

On Wednesday, March 18, 2009, about seven or eight o'clock in the morning, as I mentioned in a previous chapter, we were involved in a motor vehicle accident on our way to therapy. I was thrust forward, flipped upside down and thrown between the seats into the windshield in that accident. At the time, I had no clue that I was being turned upside down, I thought the vehicle was turning upside down. In my mind, I thought we were at this bridge section crossing over Highway 78. Every time we drove past that section, I always thought, "This is a bad spot to get in an accident because you have nowhere to go but downhill. It would be impossible to survive that drop."

I was so discombobulated to the point I thought I landed in the trunk. My head was in the windshield and parts of my face, like my lips, were on the passenger's side front window and doorframe. My neck and body were twisted. After the collision, all I heard my friend yell was "Get out the car. Get out the car." In my mind I was thinking, "Oh no, the car is going to explode." I could see and smell smoke, but was not sure what was going on at that moment. Then I wondered how I was going to get out of the car. I could not walk. I remember my right hand really hurting. I ended up crawling out of the car, hands first. It was very painful especially when my legs fell to the ground.

Once I got out of the car, I dragged myself away from the car. Everybody was asking if I was okay. I kept asking for my phone. Somebody went to the car and found my phone for me. We were in downtown Stone Mountain, so both the police station and fire department responded immediately. A police officer came to take my statement. He kept saying, "Ma'am you were lucky that you were not ejected from your vehicle with the impact of that crash." My driver was okay. She had cuts and bruises on her face, arms and legs. Her leg pushed in and cracked the dashboard under the steering wheel.

The ambulance arrived and they put me on a stretcher and put a collar around my neck. I freaked out: I am claustrophobic and I was not ready to get into another vehicle strapped down with no way out if another accident were to occur. My heart and mind were racing. I called my Godfather, Jaru, I called Martha from church and I called First-lady Morrison, the pastor's wife. I also called the therapy facility to let them know what had happened and I would not be there that morning.

While I laid on the ground, it began to drizzle a little bit. In my mind I thought, "Are they just going to keep me laying here while rain drops on my forehead?" I could not do anything about it because I was strapped down in the stretcher. I started to shiver because I was cold and scared. I asked for a blanket. Initially they said that they did not have any, but would find me one. As they lifted me, they struggled. They tilted the gurney back and forth. I panicked all over again. I know, I know: Drama Queen, right? I do not deny it.

Anyway, it appeared as if they were going to drop me and I did not want to be strapped down in the ambulance. I began to yell, "Put me down; put me down." They allowed me to ride up front, but I had to sign a waiver. I was scared to ride up front as well because I was too close to the windshield. What if there were another accident? My head would be right at that windshield again. However, I thought to myself, the lesser of two evils is the front seat in the event another accident occurred. Being strapped in would not afford me the opportunity to get myself out of the car in the event another accident took place. Besides, I did not want to be separated from my friend. We would have had to ride in two separate emergency vehicles.

I knew the Lord, but I was extremely fearful for some reason. I asked them to take us to DeKalb. I did not know that you had to specify between DeKalb Medical Decatur and Hillandale. I wanted to go to Hillandale in Lithonia, Georgia. My doctor was there and it was closer to home. Nonetheless, we ended up at DeKalb Medical in Decatur. My friend and I were separated at that point. They took me in a room and asked what my ailments were. They took some x-rays.

At the time, although my shoulder, neck and back were bothering me, my right knee and hand were throbbing. I hit my knee on the seat as I was being tossed about the vehicle. My right hand was swollen about the size of my thigh. If you know me, you know that there is nothing little about me. So, picture that.

After the x-rays, I never returned to my room. They wheeled me into the hallway with a bunch of other people. I was like, wow, this is some 'Good Times,' type of treatment here. My insurance is not good enough for privacy? Could they have at least separated us by a curtain? I saw my friend over against a wall. I asked her if she was okay. I believe she had a bad headache at the time. After the x-rays came back, they told me nothing was broken, but I was like, "No way," as big as my hand was. They told me to follow up with an orthopedic doctor. They came and wrapped my hand in the hallway. Really? In the hallway? They told me they only saw some type of shrapnel near my pinky finger. Since there was no entry point, they were not sure what it was. They also said that it had appeared on a previous x-ray and showed no changes.

We had to sit in the hallway until they brought our release papers. We signed the papers right there in the hallway. I know I paid the same amount of money for treatment as did the persons who had rooms the entire time. My friend never even got a room. They sat her in the hallway from the beginning. We were released. My friend's sister came to pick us up. The comical part, well I guess it was not comical at that time, but—I am on crutches, I cannot walk, my hand is wrapped in an ace bandage so how in the world was I supposed to hold the crutches?

I was okay leaving the hospital because they at least wheeled me to our vehicle. However, what was I going to do when I arrived home; hop on one leg? Well that is exactly how I got in the house. I had to hop on one leg and one crutch. What a sight to see. Nonetheless, I made it in the house. The next task was getting upstairs to my bedroom. To be honest with you, I really do not recall how I made it up the stairs, but I did. I waited until my mother got off from work. Then I called her.

I know some of you are probably thinking she should have been the first person I called. No, you do not know my mother. She would have left her job, even if it meant getting fired to get to me and would have spent an astronomical amount on a last minute plane ticket. I cannot remember, but I do believe I called and told my sister what happened and made her swear to secrecy. I told her I would call Mom later. Well when I called and told her, she was happy I was alive, she tripped because I had not called her sooner. The way she tripped, I told her that was why I did not call her earlier. I reassured her that I was okay and was happy that somebody else did not have to make the phone call for me.

After the Ruleys left, reality sat in. I was torn between blessing the Lord and being pissed off. I wanted to be mad, but I had to be grateful. **It could have gone another way.** My little cousin Tyesha was in an automobile accident. She got ejected from the SUV and it landed on top of her, killing her instantly. Therefore, I really had nothing to complain about, so you would think. I will say this however, for the first time in my life, I really understood about angels and the blood of Jesus. That was the only explanation to my cracking the windshield as opposed to going through it. Conversely, I began to allow the devil to whisper in my ear after this experience.

One of the issues I had was I purchased my vehicle in June 2003. I was set to make my last payment October 2009. However, I budgeted my money to pay it off by June/July. I only had about five more payments left on my car. I planned to keep that car until it just fell apart. I was so angry behind that, but I kept thinking how whatever the enemy had planned for me on that day, God and His angels blocked it. If I never fully believed in the blood and angels before, that accident made me a believer. The paramedics and firemen kept saying how lucky I was since I was not ejected from the vehicle wearing no seatbelt. I knew it was not luck, I knew we were blessed. All I could think about was, I shall live and not die to declare the glory of the Lord. Unfortunately, this one accident led to a string of events happening in my life thereafter. Thus, my birth certificate became my death certificate.

Later on, the first lie I listened to was the devil saying, "See? You are cursed. You just cannot seem to get ahead for nothing." I got angry because there it was, I had paid over $500 a month over 5 years, for this vehicle, and now I would have to start from scratch. My vehicle was in great shape and great condition. Outside of routine maintenance, the only repairs I had to do on it were the brakes. The insurance did cash out my vehicle and I searched around for weeks for a vehicle to purchase using cash. I did not want any more car notes. I decided that I was not going to get another car loan because it was time for me to start paying back my student loans. At that time, my student loan payments were $1,500 a month. That was a mortgage in and of itself. In fact, that was greater than my mortgage.

I was having problems car shopping because I had no desire for a particular automobile. I mean I used to want a BMW, but I was not a big car person in the sense of having a dream car. When I graduated from high school, I wanted an Aries K car because my name was Kem and I was born in April. Now when I think back on that foolishness, even I have to laugh at myself right now. Having said all of this, there was no particular vehicle in my spirit. All I knew was that I did not want a car because I was scared of the front seat. I needed plenty of room (distance) from me to the windshield.

It took three years after the accident to even ride in the front seat of anyone's car. I would sit in the back even if it were just the two of us. If they had smaller children, I would get in the back with their children. I was not even sure about getting another SUV because all of the ones that I was getting into had little distance from the driver's seat to the windshield. I needed something that offered distance between the glass and me. At first, the only vehicle that I saw with that type of room was the Nissan Murano. But I felt like the top of the car was coming down on me. It did not offer what I considered a lot of headroom.

It got down to the wire and I needed a new vehicle. Once the insurance policy cashed out my vehicle, they only gave me a week to look for a new one. By then my birthday was coming up and I refused to be without a vehicle for my birthday. Although the insurance company only paid for a rental car through April 8, I extended the time at least through my birthday weekend. I had never paid attention to Acura's before until my brother told me to go and check them out. I went to the Acura dealer, but of course, my credit was shot. They told me I had to wait for them to hear back from the bank. The sales representative told me he would call me back.

The next day, I was sick and left work early. I had just gotten home to lie down and the sale person called to say that I was approved and asked if I could come back to the dealership. I told him to give me an hour and I would head that way. I took an 1 ½ hour nap and drove down to Morrow, Georgia. To make a long story short, I got the loan. However, I was so excited about the loan, that I did not pay attention to the HIGH interest rate. I was more concerned with if I could afford the monthly payments over what the actual loan was costing me. Buyers beware. **Read all of the print, especially the fine print**.

THOUGHTS TO PONDER

- ❖ Do not allow the enemy cause you to go back and forth in your emotions
- ❖ The enemy's job is to plant seeds of doubt
- ❖ Agree with God quickly and stay the course
- ❖ He gives His angels charge over us
- ❖ Some blessings are in disguise

NOTES OF INSPIRATION

_____

_____

_____

_____

_____

_____

_____

_____

_____

_____

_____

_____

_____

_____

Chapter 11

FAITH AND FORECLOSURE

FAITH

April 13, 2009, I had a new car: Acura MDX with a new 5-6 year car note. Nonetheless, I had reliable transportation. I had no clue that life would take the unexpected turn it did. In the meanwhile, I was still being treated for my hand injury from the automobile accident. I had an appointment with the orthopedic doctor for my knee. He in turn looked at my hand and asked what was going on with it. I told him I had trouble with it since the accident. I told him the other doctor, from Resurgens, told me to wear the brace for support to see if it made it any better. Meanwhile, I am four weeks out from the accident. He took the brace off my hand and examined my thumb. He told me that it appears as if I had a torn ligament in my thumb. He took my thumb and moved it around. It moved in all sorts of directions. He told me that it should not bend or move beyond a certain point.

He told me that if I had a torn ligament, we needed to repair it immediately. The longer I waited, the more I risked permanent damage. I went for an MRI. It came back that I had a torn ligament in my right thumb. I would need surgery. I had been out on worker's compensation since February 19. I was supposed to return to work on March 31 from that, but since I was still having problems related to the accident, I was off until like April 7. To make a long story short, I went back to work for about two weeks or so. We scheduled the surgery for April 30, 2009.

I went out on short-term disability. During that time, I filed my taxes. I was watching Henry Fernandez's ministry on television at the time. He ministered about sustainment seed. I thought about how my savings dwindled down. I used it to supplement my worker's compensation check in order to pay the mortgage. My friend that was driving my car at the time of the accident was facing financial issues as well because she had been out of work for a while. Anyway, I sowed a sustainment seed for me and one for my friend. We both needed sustainment at that point.

Many people may not believe in seed sowing, but I am a living testimony that **when you sow, you reap a harvest.** Due to these unforeseen circumstances in my life, eventually, my savings had dwindled down. When I made my last payment in June, I contacted Bank of America to explain my situation. I told them that after that payment, I would not have enough money to supplement my income to meet the next mortgage payment. I asked what I could do to stay current. The man on the other end of the phone told me that they could not help me because I was not behind. I was like, "Excuse me, repeat that." I said, "Sir, I do not want to get behind, but I know that I cannot afford to make another payment on this loan." He repeated himself that they could not help me until I got behind.

Unfortunately, my trouble did not stop there. I was in Philadelphia at our church convention and received a phone call from my employer informing me that because I was out on workman's compensation and short-term disability that I would not get paid in

June and July. My next check would not be until August 31. I said, "And you are just calling me now about this?" Of course in my mind I thought, I would not have planned to attend that convocation had I been privy to that information. To top it off, when I arrived in Philadelphia, my rental car reservations fell through. I was stranded at the rental car place. I did know how to get from there to the convention in Ben Salem. I contacted my friend, Vincent Woolard. He picked me up and dropped me off at Freedom Christian Bible Fellowship, not at the convention.

To make matters worse, 2009 was the year that Gwinnett County Public Schools decided to cut our salaries. I went backwards in terms of my pay. 1) We did not get a raise; 2) They furloughed us three days and took the furlough amount out of our August-December checks; and 3) They cut the additional 10% I was receiving as a National Board Certified Teacher. Wow. But I heard Bishop Hudson singing in my ear, "I don't care what the devil says, my life just got better. I win. He loses." I trusted the sustainment seed that was sown.

So now, I have this new extremely high car payment that I could afford prior to the pay cut. I have the same amount of bills that I had prior to the pay cut, but I had no way to make ends meet. I thought the car accident was something, but it just went downhill from there. In the midst of all of that which took place, I felt a pull in my spirit to leave my current ministry. That was an extremely hard decision because I loved the ministry and the people. We were such a tight knit family. Every time I told someone that knew me I played the keyboard, they would laugh. Even my previous pastors were shocked.

One Sunday, both my mom, Bettie, and Godmother, Mrs. Ruley, came to church to visit. I was playing the keyboard. I started playing this song and I messed up. I said, "Wait a minute. Hold up. Let me start over." Both my mom and Mrs. Ruley were so embarrassed. They both put their heads down in shame. I saw their faces while I was playing and was so tickled inside, I almost messed up again. It took everything out of me to not jump off that keyboard and start rolling on the floor laughing. They could not believe I did that; but that was the type of ministry I was in at the time. We all were growing together. **They understood that I was not perfect but was willing to lend my gift to the Lord while He perfected it.** By the way, I did get better with time.

That is the reason why it was so hard to leave. I was not sure where to go. I fasted and prayed to make sure I was led by the Holy Spirit. There was this church that I passed every day on my way home from the Ruleys' house. Sometimes, I would pass there late at night and see cars in the parking lot. I would think to myself, they church like Prayer and Faith in Chicago. One day either I called the church or went online to see what time services were held. When I saw a 7AM service, I was like, oh yeah. At that time, the 2nd service was held at 10AM. I will never forget. I went and the message was, "This is My Defining Moment." I knew that was God. Not only that, but they were starting a weight-loss challenge called Fit and Fabulous. I asked if I could be a part without being a member. Several members were friendly to me and were ranting and raving about the ministry.

I did not join right away because I had not met with my previous pastor. I did not just want to leave without saying anything. For whatever reason, we were just not able to connect. Eventually, I felt led to connect with the new ministry during August. It was what they called August Connection Month. I flew to Minneapolis Friday, August 7 for my Doctoral Ceremony. I graduated that Saturday and joined the ministry that Sunday, August 9. That was truly a defining moment in my life. It was a new chapter in my life. Sometime when you are led to leave a ministry, it is not always because something bad transpired. Sometimes it is about what God wants to do in your life. I have been blessed to have had awesome leaders in my life. Each one took me as far as God allowed them. The next one picked up where the previous one left off.

Meanwhile, financially I was sinking. I was a month behind in my mortgage, 3 months behind on my car and behind on my other bills. Eventually, my lights were cut off. I did not tell a soul, but I was living by candle light. I would try to rush home after work to get there before dark so that I could get prepared for the next day. Sometimes I stayed at the Ruleys' until it was time to go to bed. In the mornings, I lit a candle and took a shower. Eventually, my phones were disconnected. I know that God was doing something in my life because usually I would have been depressed and asking God why. But this time, I had a peace about my situation. I knew it was just temporary. I was grateful it was just me and I was not responsible for anyone else, like children at that time. It moved me to intercede on behalf of single parents. I went to work and church as usual and nobody knew otherwise. I decided to fast my way through since I could not cook anyway.

Eventually, as I began to get paid again, I started to catch up on my bills little by little. However, I was not able to catch up on my mortgage. Around October/November I received correspondence from the bank that they were planning to foreclose on my house. I went to a N.A.C.A. event and begin to work with them. My house was set to foreclose February, 2010; however, since I was working with N.A.C.A. they postponed the foreclosure. When I started getting paid again, I sent a payment to Bank of America. They refused to take the payment and said that I had to pay the entire past due balance. I explained my story once again to them, sent in letters and the whole nine yards, but to no avail. I was not able to get assistance from them.

FORECLOSURE

Meanwhile, I worked with N.A.C.A. This time my house was set to foreclose in March. Again, it got postponed. Since they were still reviewing my file, they said they would postpone it again. Finally it was set to foreclose in April. I spoke with them the Friday before it was set to foreclose. The lady told me that they cannot postpone it anymore because it had already been postponed twice. I explained to the lady what was going on, how I was working with N.A.C.A. and asked how they could just foreclose on my loan if they have not even reviewed my file and rendered a decision. So the lady told me that she would look into it and postpone it one more time. That was Friday April 3, 2010. I was out on spring break the following week. It was during this time I accepted my call to travel to Cape Town, South Africa, on my first international mission's trip. That Monday I was led to have a mission's party and charge people $10 to come to help support the mission's trip. The party was scheduled for Saturday, April 10, my birthday. That Monday, I sent out invitations.

I also had an appointment with N.A.C.A. via phone that Tuesday. In speaking with N.A.C.A., I learned my house had gone into foreclosure earlier that day. I could not believe it. I was livid. I began to call the bank and was switched from one person to the next and so forth. I could not get any resolution. Discouraged, I went to Wal-Mart and purchased storage bins to begin packing. I tripped because I was scheduled to have my party Saturday, and as of that day, I no longer had a house. I began to pack. That Wednesday, I went to Bible study. When I went home that evening, I continued packing and the Holy Spirit told me not to pack another thing and not to purchase another box or storage bin.

At that point, I took off my grave clothes and begin to prepare for my party. I told my family what was going on. They thought I was crazy. But that is when God begin to minister to me that I needed to have Noah-like faith. I asked God, "What is that?" He explained that if Noah would have had a "what if," there would have been no ark. Noah was asked to build something he had never seen or heard of before because it was about to rain. He did not know what rain was either. All Noah knew was that he heard from God. He obeyed. There was no time for *what if* it did not rain; *what if* people did not believe him. That was the place where God wanted me. I did not have time for what if they came to take my house and I was not packed, ready to move. I stayed right there in that house three years mortgage free.

I had the party on Saturday as planned and we had a ball. The food was great. I gamed them to death and introduced them to a game called Mafia. I started a Mafia craze at Harvest. That Sunday, I shared with my pastor what was going on to get his opinion of the situation. I was standing on faith and did not care what it or I looked like to other people. Even he kind of looked at me like I was crazy, but he said stand on the word of the Lord. Hope for the best, plan for the worst. Meanwhile, about a month later, I received a sheriff's note on my door to go to court. I filed what they called "the answer." The court date they initially gave me was for the exact same time I would be in South Africa.

I explained to them that I would be out of the country during that time. I had to fill out more paper work to request an extension. They told me they would notify me of the judge's decision. For some reason, I did not care what the judge said, I was on my way to South Africa and they could do what they wanted. I told my pastor that as well. I know he thought I was crazy. But God told me I was not going to get put out of my house and I believed him. The next day after I told my pastor that I was going to South Africa regardless, I received a call from the court that my date had been changed to the Tuesday after I returned from my trip.

I went to Cape Town, served and had the experience of a lifetime. Not once did I think about that house. I came back to America, went to court and they gave me seven days to get out. I kept calling the bank and calling their attorney's office trying to get someone to revisit my file. I found an error in the calculations on the paperwork. They kept telling me that I did not qualify for a modification based on my salary. I did not understand that because, although there was a decrease in my salary, I still made more than I did when I first purchased the house four years prior. Initially, nobody would listen to me. Finally, the attorney's office agreed to give me until the end of the month to move.

What is ironic about all of this is I even sent emails to the White House, called my state representatives and still did not get anywhere with this situation. Below is a response to an email I sent to the White House.

The White House - Presidential Correspondence
<noreply-WHPC@whitehouse.gov>

5/11/10

to me

Dear Kemberly McKenzie:

Thank you for writing. I have heard from Americans who are unemployed, burdened by high medical bills, having difficulty paying their mortgage, or dealing with the loss of their home, and I understand the daunting challenges they face.

Today, even as our economy recovers, many individuals and families are still struggling to stay in their homes. As part of my Administration's comprehensive plan to stabilize the housing market, the Making Home

Affordable Program is helping responsible families avoid foreclosure by making payments more affordable and sustainable. While many Americans have received help, far too many still cannot refinance their mortgages or obtain loan modifications. We have made significant improvements to our plan, and I encourage you to learn more by visiting the Making Home Affordable website.

Along with these changes, we have strengthened the program with a simpler, faster application process so borrowers can modify their payments and avoid foreclosure. For Americans whose homes have lost value, my Administration's plan improves refinancing opportunities. We are also requiring more accountability and transparency from participating mortgage servicers, and have published servicers' monthly progress reports. I will continue to meet with my economic advisors every day to make sure we are doing all we can to get Americans the help they need.

For assistance with a home foreclosure or to find a local housing counselor, I encourage you to call your mortgage servicer directly, speak with a housing specialist at 1-888-995-HOPE, or contact the Department of Housing and Urban Development at 1-800-569-4287. You can also visit www.hud.gov/foreclosure or www.MakingHomeAffordable.gov. If you have lost your home and are looking for housing assistance please visit www.HUD.gov. Information on jobs, health benefits, and other public resources available to those in need can be found by calling 1-800-FEDINFO or visiting: www.usa.gov.

The road ahead is difficult, but as we recover from this crisis, we can once again secure the American Dream for ourselves and future generations.

Sincerely,
Barack Obama

To be a part of our agenda for change, join us at <u>www. WhiteHouse.gov</u>

Meanwhile, I continued to contact Bank of America every day to plead my case. Finally, the day before I was supposed to be out of the house, I got this lady on the phone from Bank of America who listened to me. She saw the mistake that I was talking about and agreed to have somebody look into it. She postponed my moving date indefinitely. That was the end of June. Prior to all of this, I had contacted HUD and opened a case with them to do an investigation. Eventually, after calling both the bank and their attorney's office I learned that my new move-out date was scheduled for Wednesday, August 11, 2010.

All of this time, I still had not packed anything. God said I was not going to get put out. I believed him. I had Noah-like faith. In the interim, I would continue to call Bank of America regularly to get some type of resolve and to get my house back. I spoke with someone on that Saturday, August 7, who agreed to pass my case along to a supervisor for review. He told me he would call me back on Monday, August 9. That was our first day back to school with the students. I was led to check my email, which is something I usually do not do. I had an email from the Home Owners' Association. At first, I ignored the email. I thought they were just reminding me of my HOA fees; however, I felt led to go back and read the email. It read as follows:

From: Jacqcy <jackieraws@att.net>
Subject: Urgent!!! re: 6216 Lake Valley Point
To: KemberlyMcKenie@gmail.com
Cc: "raiommunities" <raimunities@msn.com>
Date: Monday, August 9, 2010, 3:32 PM

Hello Ms. McKenzie,

I just received a phone call from Parkview's Landscaper. He stated the Marshall's are in the process of putting all your household goods, furniture and personal belongings in your front yard.

I do not have a phone number on file to contact you regarding this urgent matter.

PLEASE CONFIRM YOU RECEIVED THIS IMPORTANT EMAIL.

Thanks,

Jackie
Community Association Manager,
HOA

Can you image being at work reading this email? My heart dropped to the floor. I went to grab my phone and saw that my neighbor had been trying to reach me. I called her and she confirmed what was taking place. I pushed the emergency button in my classroom for an administrator. They never responded. I then took my class to the cafeteria. I informed my principle that I had an emergency at home and needed to leave. He told me to speak with my assistant principal. I went to my assistant principal and told him the same thing. I even told him the situation at hand. He told me that he needed to go and find my department chair. He never came back. I proceeded to my department chair's office to look for them. They were not there. Now generally the procedure is you go to the department chair first, then assistant principal, then principal. So clearly, I was getting the run around. I just left.

I called people to get someone over to my house. I cannot remember if I contacted Elder King or my brother, Jarun first, but I spoke with both of them. They both said they would go over there. I called Bank of America and got nowhere with them. I called HUD and she did not know what was going on and said she would call me back. All I thought about was God said I would not be put out of my house. I purposed in my heart that they would have to arrest me that night because I was not leaving.

Before I could get home, The supervisor of the company that was putting my things out of the house called to apologize to me. She said, "Ms. McKenzie, I am so sorry. I got a call and this was a mistake. We were just following orders." She informed me that they were putting my stuff back into my house and fixing my lock. She said they were on their way to Home Depot to get a new lock. She also said that she told the workers to put everything back into my house and to at least set up my bed. She further explained how she knew that was devastating and at least I would have my bed to lay in when I got home.

I got home and pulled up to my brother snapping. The men tried to steal my washer and dryer. Elder King was there. My brother was trying to tell me they were trying to take my washer and dryer. I walked into chaos. So I got my brother calm and I go inside my house to see what was going on. Meanwhile, the lady from HUD calls to tell me it was a mistake and she does not know why they were there. They were still reviewing my file. I walked in my house and the place looked ransack I could not believe it. But I told myself to stay calm. God's hand was in it. The men had piled everything into the garage. I told them to put my stuff back into my house. That is where they got it from. I told them they should not have touched it in the first place. I told them I did not live in my garage. I parked my car in my garage.

The men told me that they were finished moving everything after they put my washer and dryer back in the house. They told me that they moved out; they do not move in. I called their supervisor and told her what was going on. Two of the men jumped in the truck and left. The supervisor made them return. She commanded they put my possessions back in my house. They said that they would only put my belongings back in the house on the main floor.

I noticed empty water bottles and fruit cups all over the place. I checked my refrigerator. All the fruit cups were gone. A half of case of water remained. I barely had money to purchase lunch for the week and these men had helped themselves to my food and drinks in the refrigerator. I called the supervisor back again and told her what happened. Not only that, my money on the counter was missing. They claimed that the Sheriff took it. Anyway, the supervisor asked how much I had spent on groceries and I told her. She made them come back to my house and pay me. I was livid. The nerve of them. In order to get my stuff out of the house, they opened my sheets on the floor. They put my things in the middle of the sheets. They dragged the sheets outside onto the lawn. My GOOD sheets had grass and dirt stains, in addition to holes in them.

At the end of the day, I threw everything off my futon onto the floor and I just laid there and cried. On one hand, I was happy because God came through for me; on the other hand, many of my things were destroyed in the process. I kept going back to the word of the Lord; I will not be put out of my house. As I lay there, I began to question God. I reminded him that He said I would not be put out, but asked what did He call that? He reminded me that I was laying my head on my futon, in my house. I began to magnify and praise His name. I took a nap, got up and got myself together and went to church for Monday night prayer. After prayer, I told my pastor what happened. When I got to the point that they had put all my stuff out of my house, he looked somewhat disappointed as if he believed God with me. Then I told him the remainder of the story and his countenance changed.

I continued to fight for my house. I kept trying to prove to Bank of America that there was an error with the calculations. I requested to get my house back. I wrote all sorts of letters, tried to hire an attorney, but nobody wanted to touch it with a 10 foot pole because it was Bank of America. I finally found an attorney that would take the case, but she ended up not working out. In 2012, I was set to go back to Cape Town, South Africa for the 3rd time. I got a letter that I must appear in court again. Mind you, I still lived in my house 2 years after the foreclosure and 3 years from the time I made my last mortgage payment. Now will you believe in sowing seed? **God sustained me.** However, this is where I believed I made my mistake. When we went before the judge, he asked if we had been through mediation and their representative stated no. He gave us the opportunity to meet first and then come back before him.

I met with the representatives. I had all of my documentation. She bargained with me. She said the judge would only give me 7 days, but she would extend the time. I told her I planned to travel to South Africa within the next week or so. She agreed to give me at least 14 days, but could not guarantee anything after that. She did agree to notify me to let me know when I needed to be out of the property.

I was tired of the fight and decided to take the deal and vacate the premises. We went back before the judge and he asked if I agreed to the terms. I told him yes. At that moment, I felt something in me, as if I was giving up. I felt like I should have at least presented my case before the judge and let him make the decision. I kept hearing "the heart of the king is in the hand of the Lord... for him to turn whithersoever way He will" (Proverbs 21:1). What was done was already done. I fought for that house since 2009. It was 2012.

Right before I left to go to South Africa, I received a letter from the attorney's office that if I agreed to be out by July 11, 2012 they would give me cash for keys in the event that I left the house in good condition. This was good timing because I would have been back from Africa a week before I had to move. Before I went to Africa, I packed my house. I also looked for a place to live. A few days before I left I was approved for an apartment (a 2 bedroom, 2 bathroom loft). I told you I had fascinations with lofts. What is funny about the cash for keys is, I asked about that in the beginning of the foreclosure process and was told I did not qualify. Look at God. Won't He do it? Again, I lived in the house mortgage free 3 full years and 2 years after foreclosure. I moved out July 7, 2012.

To top this story off, I was part of the national foreclosure fraud. I received two small settlements. Of course they were nowhere near what I felt I should have gotten, but I did not have to get anything at all. I was grateful. Even after the settlement, I still fought to get my house back because it was still unoccupied. I finally got a letter from Bank of America's attorney in December of 2013 telling me that although I was part of the foreclosure process that they did not do anything wrong and they were not rescinding their previous decision. I decided to close that chapter of my life then and not bring it into another year. I decided to K.E.M. (Keep Everything Moving).

THOUGHTS TO PONDER

❖ What appears to be the end, may very well be the beginning
❖ Do not be afraid to let go and move on
❖ Forgive and live (yourself, others and God if necessary)
❖ Remove the "what if" from your thoughts
❖ Be steadfast in your faith regardless
❖ What is impossible with man is possible with God
❖ The ark was needed for the flood
❖ If it is possible for you, there would be no need for God to do the impossible

NOTES OF INSPIRATION

_____

_____

_____

_____

_____

_____

_____

_____

_____

_____

_____

_____

_____

_____

Chapter 12

REJECTION AND REBELLION

THE SPIRIT OF REJECTION

When you do not know who you are and recognize that God does not make any junk, you are wrestling with a broken identity. If we are in the King's bloodline then we are entitled to blessings. Some of us know God and have been with Him for years, yet we settle for a low place: Lodebar (a place of desertion: no pasture, no hope, total desolation). That is what happened to Jonathan's son, Mephibosheth. He was crippled and hiding in Lodebar. He had an identity problem. He considered himself a dead dog. Read II Samuel 9 for the full story. Broken identity is linked to low self-esteem. We then self-sabotage. This is a sign that we do not love ourselves. If you bend down long enough, eventually your back will hurt.

I learned from being at The Harvest Tabernacle Church that all of my issues could be traced to unmet needs, unresolved issues and/ or unhealed hurt from my childhood or past. I thought I was okay. I learned that I had a lot of junk in me that needed to be gutted out. For years I had been operating in rejection and rebellion which open the door for the spirit of Jezebel to rule and reign in my life. For the record, Jezebel is a controlling spirit.

Because my past was what I considered beyond my control, I was determined to control my future, no matter what it took. I had a thing about people hollering & yelling at me and telling me what to do. Although the word was good and my connection with the ministry was my defining moment, Initially I did not care for Apostle Jennings' pastoral ways. I felt he was rough and hard on me like my mother was. By the way, they get along so well. I use to tell God, let me do what I need to do so that I can get out of Georgia. I was leaving Georgia every 6 months. I felt every time I went to church, he fussed at me, in particular (Jezebel). Every chance he got, he reminded me I was not connected. It was not until this last time I tried to leave Georgia, the Holy Spirit revealed to me that I had been processing him, the ministry and Georgia through the eyes of rejection. This caused me to operate in rebellious, Jezebelic ways without my even knowing or trying.

I remember Apostle Jennings told me how rebellious I was. I did not see it. I always felt like he misconstrued my actions. But one day he said, "You know Dr. McKenzie, even unknown rebellion is still rebellion." Wow. That was an eye opener for me. See, sometimes we can operate under a spirit so long until we do not even recognize it. You can get to a point like I did where you start not to even recognize yourself. I will never forget this as long as I live. I had been offered a job as an assistant principal back in Chicago. I had been waiting seven years to become an assistant principal. I never even applied for this particular job. One Bible study my pastor told us to speak our name into the atmosphere and that doors were going to open. Promotion was in the house. Our resumes were going to be put at the top.

A day or so later my friend, Mike, called me and said they had an assistant principal position open. Based on his recommendations the principal wanted to interview and hire me. The interview was just for formality. I was like, "Oh wow God you worked fast this time." Initially they wanted me to fly out to Chicago for the interview. I had just returned from South Africa and moved into my apartment. I told him let me pray about it. All I could see was six figures. All my financial woes would be over. That would definitely make up for the $20,000 pay cut I took relocating from Chicago to Atlanta. So I felt the urge to go. I called my pastor to inform him about the job offer. I was asking him what he thought, but the reality of it was, that was my way of letting him know I was moving.

His response was what is the Holy Spirit telling you? I said: leave. He goes on and on about how the Holy Spirit he knows would not uproot somebody before the process is complete. He continued in that vein for a while in essence to say, God is not through with me here. When I hung up the phone, I thought to myself that did not go the way I planned. I expected him to release me. In all honesty, I really thought my pastor did not care for me that much. I felt as if I frustrated his anointing and irritated his spirit. It appeared that he always had something negative to say about me or towards me (deception). He would make these faces that I read to mean, "When are you going to leave this church" (perception)? In my mind, I was getting out of his hair and off his nerves.

Well I called Mike back to say I wanted to take the position, but it was bad timing. I explained how I had just returned from South Africa, moved and started a position at a new school in the fall. I explained I would not be able to fly out there right then. He said he understood and we both talked about how timing is everything. The next week, I got a call from him saying the principal really wanted to hire me and asked if I could do a phone interview. Well that was my answer there. I figured, hey, if I turned the position down and it came back around to me, then I most definitely am supposed to take it; not to mention six figures.

I went to church and I told my pastor that I turned the position down but they offered it to me again. I told him that I was taking the position and that my interview was within the next day or so. I was so happy. I felt a release in my spirit. I thought he would be happy too because I was getting out of his hair. Well his response shocked me. He said, "Didn't I tell you not to take that position?"

I said, "No, sir. You said what did the Holy Spirit tell me? I said the Holy Spirit was saying six figures."

He said, "You know, it's not always about the money, Dr. McKenzie."

I said, "Yes I know, but I am tired of the struggle." He asked about the weather and my knees. I told him with six figures, I could buy coats and boots and clothes. He just shook his head. Then I explained to him how all this time I thought I was okay. It was not until I got to Harvest that I understood that I needed to be delivered and fully healed. It was there I learned healing is like an onion. It has layers to it depending upon how deep-seated the hurt is. Although some healing had taken place over the years there was still some residue.

I mentioned to him that I did not have the opportunity to serve Bishop Hudson right. I explained that I did not know that I was rebellious and acted like a Jezebel when I served under his ministry. I told him I used to want to go back and serve under him better once I came face to face with who I had become. I resolved that since I was at Harvest, I would serve him the best I could, instead. Since the opportunity presented itself for me to return to Chicago, I wanted to make things right. He told me a story. The story he told me was a simple one, but it changed my life. I will explain what the story meant to me after I share it. He began to talk to me about a rose and flowers. He talked about when a rose opens up and fully blooms to its fullest dimension how beautiful and useful the rose is. He discussed how that was when it served its purpose. He talked about the effects of the rose when it reaches its fullest dimension/potential. At first in my mind I was thinking, he has no idea I do not even like flowers. Nonetheless, I stuck with him to the end of his story.

He went on to explain that when he bought his wife flowers, especially roses, he did not purchase them from the grocery store. They did not leave their roses in the soil long enough. He explained how he went to a certain flower shop to purchase his roses. The ones from the grocery store did not open up to their fullest dimension or last long. The ones from the flower shop, he explained, were left in the ground long enough so that when they bloomed, they reached their fullest dimension and they lasted longer. Not only that, they looked and smelled better than the other roses. They did what they were created/designed to do.

I was like, wow. I just heard an entire dissertation on dirt and roses because I'm moving to Chicago. Nonetheless, I was tremendously blessed by it as simple as it may have seemed. It was quite profound in essence. I got two messages from that story:

1. I am a rose and need to stay rooted and grounded long enough so that I can reach my fullest potential. Then and only then can I be as beautiful and effective as God intended for me to be. He used to always tell us in "Ministers' Training Classes," to allow God to complete the work in us so that when we went before the people we would affect them, not infect them. That was profound to me. That was what he was saying in this rose story. Die to yourself long enough and allow God to complete the work so that you can be all that He intended you to be; then you will be able to effectively impact the world.

2. He did not want me to leave. All that just baffled me because I just knew he was not going to ask me to leave the ministry, but was waiting for me to get fed up enough myself and just leave. Again, deception and perception were wreaking havoc in my life. In his saying it was not my time to leave, he was also saying, "Stay. You belong here." As dirty as it may seem, this is your ground of dirt. At that moment, I felt that he was taking ownership for me as a pastor after God's own heart. He did not allow personality, or fault to cloud the work God was trying to complete in my life. He saw beyond my rejection, rebellion, offense and hurt. He saw the end from the beginning: a beautiful rose, effective and operating in my fullest potential.

Although it was heart-felt, at the time six figures were still calling my name. So I went to get my hair done to prepare for the phone interview. I even laid my interview suit out. I told my beautician that. She got so tickled. I told her I planned to move to Chicago in August. I told her this was perfect because I just moved and had not had a chance to unpack anything as of yet. I left her house, headed home to prepare for the interview. I was driving on a back road: Rogers Lake. I will never forget it. The Holy Spirit began to minister to me and tell me no, don't take that job. I was driving and talking to myself at the same time. I said, "Get thee behind me Satan, six figures are at stake." I heard the Holy Spirit say no again. It was the No I was familiar with hearing when I would ask God about a particular man I was seeing and if it was His will or not. It was that same kind of No.

I felt something in the pit of my stomach. I cannot explain it. It was like disappointment, hopelessness and excitement all wrapped up in one. I was disappointed because if he was saying no, that meant I had to stay in Georgia longer. I used to say all the time I hated Georgia because it was purely a place of test and trials. I was hopeless because I saw my car paid off, student loans paid off and myself dressing better. Now I thought back to the struggle and the grind. On the other hand, I was excited because He answered me. I asked God from the very beginning if it was His will or not to take this job. I prayed for Him to shut the door if it was not His will. Since the door swung open twice, I thought, it must be God. Either way, I was excited because **He loved me enough to not allow me to miss Him.** He also loved me enough to connect me with the right covering. He loved me enough to not allow me to self-sabotage and pull myself up from the dirt too soon.

Not only did He tell me not to take the job, He began to minister to me and showed me how I had processed my experience with Apostle Jennings, The Harvest Tabernacle Church, and Georgia through the eyes of rejection and hurt. He gave me a glimpse of how strong that spirit was rooted in me. By then I had pulled over on the side of the road, hands lifted and boo-hooing. When God was through with me, all I could do was repent and receive. I got myself together after a while. It was a few minutes before the interview was to take place. I called my contact and told him that God told me NO; it's not my time. I told him God was not finished with me in Georgia. I could tell my friend was upset. I am sure he stuck his neck out there for me to get that position and I turned it down twice. He was not as upset as I initially was. I saw those six figures just fly right out of my car window.

After I spoke to Mike, the Holy Spirit continued to minister to me on the side of the road. Next, I was led to call Apostle Jennings. I shared with him all the Holy Spirit revealed to me. I apologized to him for acting the way I did all those years. He said surely this is the Holy Spirit. Then he spoke healing over my life. He said because I exposed the enemy and confessed, I gave up the ground and that God was healing me. I felt so light after that. I looked in the mirror and I even looked a little lighter in complexion; if that could happen to someone of my hue. I reached a level of peace that I had not known before that day. I begin to even see myself differently.

I will not be telling the whole truth if I do not say that from time to time, I had thoughts about that salary. I started my new job and ran smack dab into the devil. Of course, I thought, I know I did not give up six figures to deal with this bull on this job. That story is for another chapter in another book. To make a long story short, I thought God was going to bless me in my new school and give me the assistant principal position that was vacant. It did not work like that. Instead, I got written up by the interim principal and ended up having to file a grievance against her. On top of that, God made me withdraw the grievance and apologize to her when she was the one wrong. He told me, "The battle was not mine; it was His." So **I had to suck it up and K.E.M.** Shortly after that, the interim principal called me in a meeting and apologized to me. She told me she had mistreated me and would not have done to others what she did to me. Saints, the Holy Spirit does not lie. It may seem like a hard pill to swallow at the time, but TRUST AND OBEY. I Promise: **God has your best interest at heart even when it does not seem like it.** Not only that, I got an email from Mike, the guy who set me up with the assistant principal position in Chicago. It read as follows:

Michael <mive@hotmail.com>
to me

The more I learn about this principal the more I know God was looking out for you. Making the move to Chicago would have been a terrible one for you. Every week something new *scares* this man. He has taken the Dean of Curriculum and put him back in the classroom, Dean of Attendance, back to the classroom, and one more person who was in charge of running night school, professional developments activities for teachers, recruiting new teachers, running new teacher *mentoring* program, she did a lot for the school, he put them all back in the classroom because rumors had it the faculty didn't like these people. It really is a political mess. He feels two Spanish A.P.'s will make him good with the LSC and teachers. So I have been ask to *step* down. Sometimes life just stinks.

Thanks again for the prayers
Michael

SPIRT OF REBELLION

Everybody at some point has lowered their expectations, gotten distracted, allowed impatience and lack of faith to cause them to do, be or act in ways unbecoming to them, especially if you consider yourself a saint of the Most High. That once was me. I allowed a man to take advantage of me for the sake of companionship and self-worth. I am about to become more vulnerable in this book to expose how the enemy preys on the minds of silly women who have not fully embraced who God deemed for us to be: a Holy Nation, Royal Priesthood, Chosen Generation called forth to declare His Glory; fearfully and wonderfully made by God.

I had waited and waited on God for a husband, so I thought. All along, He was waiting on me to get myself together. Anyway,

I became disheartened. I let rejection ride my back so long and so much that I had moved into an area of rebellion. This is my story of a fool not in Love. Thanks be unto God who always causes us to triumph. I had to go to a low place to recognize that I was seated in a high place all along. Once God showed me how rejection was ruling my life, I was able to see myself out of this next situation I, Kemberly Elaine, got myself into. I broke all the rules and made all of the mistakes in a past relationship that I must tell the truth so that others can be free. It is imperative for me to tell my story to keep other young girls, and older women for that matter, from falling into the same trap. Do not allow not getting your way; cause you to go against the Word of God.

Foolishness – I slept with a man on my 1ˢᵗ time meeting him. I know Crazy!!!! That was after being celibate for yeeaarrss. I lost my virginity at the age of 27. Fornication was not my thing. The question is WHY? There are several reasons I could give. You have read as I unfolded my past to you and I am sure by now you read some of my craziness. However, for now, the answer is simple, low self-Esteem. I hate to admit this and it will be the first time publically admitting it, let alone facing up to it, but I, Kemberly Elaine McKenzie, with my associate's degree, bachelor's degree, three masters' degrees and a PhD, struggled in the area of low self-esteem. Even as I write, further deliverance is taking place as tears stream down my face. Unfortunately, **it hurts to admit, but it is the truth anyhow.**

I knew from day one that I was not his type and neither he mine, but that did not stop me. I was intrigued. My pastor prophesied to me that God was going to send me a mate, but he was not going to be like these thugs that I was attracted to and liked. I have to admit that I was highly offended. I do not like thugs. No offense, I do not like rap and sagging pants either. Not that you have to rap to be a thug, but you get the point. It was not until I sat down to write this chapter of the book that I had an epiphany. It was not so much the person being a thug as it was allowing them to treat me in thuggish ways. Regrettably, I allowed low self-esteem to lower my standards and expectations.

Low Self-Esteem - Although he professed Christ, he was a man of the world with worldly ways, ideas, principles and theology. He laid down the law to me from day one. He gave me plenty of reasons to "Run Forrest, Run," but low self-esteem took the lead on this one. God made so many ways of escape through that one-two hour conversation, that I had no reason to even like this man, entertain him or even go over to his house later that evening and SLEEP with him. Again, the more I write, the more deliverance is taking place as the tears flow, but I have to get this out to be completely transparent and help free others. As this man talked to me, 1) I knew he was screwed up in terms of relationships from the beginning; 2) I knew he had no respect for women because he was screwed up; and 3) I knew if he had no respect for women, then he would not have any respect for me. I knew these three things going forward. Following, I am going to share the things he communicated with me at the very beginning on day one, but not necessarily in this order:

A. "I don't care what you do when you are not with me, where you go or who you are with, all I care about is how you treat me when you are in my presence. " What is that saying ladies? Well just flip it around: he can go wherever he wants, with whom he wants and do whatever he wants with other women, as long as he treats you right when he is in your presence. "That's a negative Houston." My saved, sanctified, filled with the precious Holy Ghost, self, allowed that.

I allowed myself to play by his rules and got caught up in that game. I did everything possible to make sure when this man was in my presence, he felt comfortable. We felt comfortable in each other's presence. Neither of us brought any drama. As a matter of fact, we had such a good time when we were together it was scary. We were argue free! Why? Because I catered to him. After only knowing this man for one week, I repeat, one week, I allowed this man to come to my house. That is definitely a no, no; especially when you are single and live alone. Do not do it. Keep your guard up in that respect.

B. He told me he believed in becoming friends first, then you get engaged. At that point, that is when you become exclusive; and then you get married. What kind of buffoonery is that? It sounds like afraid to commit to me. I spoke with my Godfather about this and his response was, "He's smart Kem. He is not putting all of his eggs in one basket." So basically this means he can see and sleep with as many people as he wants because he is not committed until he is engaged. The guy even backed that statement up later down the road by saying, "Kem, when you take a woman off the market, you have to be serious about her because you put her at a disadvantage."

He encouraged me to date other men, let other men take me out and show me a good time because I deserve it. Let them pay my bills. My question was, "And what will you be doing in the meanwhile, if everyone else is doing what you should be doing for me?" In the beginning of the relationship, he continued to tell me over and over again, until I spend some real money on you… I mean like a ring. Ladies, when they tell you things like this from the door, believe them and run.

Okay, one day I caught myself being nice to him. I knew he liked almond milk and cereal as a snack. Since he was spending the night periodically, and I definitely was not in a position to share my ration with him, I saw some milk and cereal on sale. I purchased it so that at least his stomach would not growl in the middle of the night. When I told him that I had a surprise for him and told him what it was, his response was, "Don't be trying to make me comfortable at your house." Ooh wee. Well naturally, I was prone to take a lot of crap off of people; perhaps it is that mercy gift God so graciously endowed me with. Any who, the 'sister girl' in me came out. I was ticked off. First of all, I could barely afford to feed myself in that season of my life; what little I did have, I tried to share it with him, and that was the thanks I got? You know Kemberly Elaine took that food right back to the grocery store and got my money back. Why was I forsaking myself to please this man? Low self-esteem.

All along, this man told me and showed me he was non-committal. However, my foolish self-wanted to believe I just needed to give him and the relationship a chance to evolve. After all, it had only been a few weeks. I wanted to believe that we had to take our time to get to know each other, although he showed and told me who he was in the beginning. I wanted to believe that once he saw I was not like the others, that he could trust me. Then he would not have a problem committing prior to engagement. He would see how kind, caring and compassionate I was. He would see he could come home to a peaceful, drama free environment. Unfortunately, what that created was an atmosphere for me to be used and frustrated. When I finally spoke up about it, he asked why I had to go and mess up our arrangement.

Loneliness - I and my home became convenient for him. Not speaking up when things bothered me, for fear of pushing him away, allowed him to think that what he was doing was okay. It sent the message that you could come and go as you please. You could go all weekend without contacting me, call on Sunday evenings to come over and spend a night. My house was closer to his Monday morning appointment; therefore, convenient. When I allowed that to take place without speaking up, it sent the message 'do whatever' I will be right here waiting with open arms. That is what I did. However, that was not how I felt. Inside, I was furious and felt used, taken for granted. It was not what I wanted, but it was what I allowed. I settled for it. The question became, why did I make it so comfortable and convenient for that man? Why did I allow him to treat me any kind of way and accepted it? LONELINESS!

I was lonely and he was my entertainment. I know further deliverance is taking place even as I write, because every time I become vulnerable and admit the truth, the devil is exposed. I cannot control the tears. I never really had to seriously admit to anyone or myself that I was lonely. Admitting to it and putting it on paper for the world to see allows God to expose the enemy and strip him of the grip he had on me through the different spirits that were working against me, within me. None of what I wrote was pre-planned. God is literally giving me word for word as I type. Pastor Stephanie prophesied to me that as I wrote the book and wrote it down, whatever had me bound would lose me. **Because I am being set free through my obedience in telling the world how the enemy held me captive, I know that everyone who reads this book will be set free by whatever has them bound.** God is willing and able. Accept your freedom in him.

Just to recap, two weapons that the enemy tries to bind us with are rejection and rebellion. When these two spirits get together, they wreak havoc. They will have you acting out of character. Other spirits like low self-esteem and loneliness creep through that opened door. I will not deal with these spirits in great details in this book. However, right now it is all about exposing the enemy.

C. When I said the Bible says to flee fornication, he said, "People misinterpret that scripture." He said, "What God was saying was that we should not sleep around because that is how we spread diseases throughout the land and kill off the population which affects the kingdom." Regardless of the purpose, that scripture, that verse, was cut and dry. There were no shades of grey or room for misinterpretation: 'flee fornication.' It means run from it. Again, God had made a way of escape for me and instead of running from it; I ran smack dab into it later that night. All the while we were having this conversation, I made up in my mind that I would never see or talk to this man ever again after that night. I thought to myself, he is definitely coo coo for *Cocoa Puffs*. Nonetheless, I ran to him and not from him. Why? LOVE!

Looking for Love in All the Wrong Places - I slept with him that very same night regardless of all the signs and warnings. I knew better. To make matters worse, I was already home perturbed by our previous conversation when he called to invite me to his house. I kept saying, crazy. I knew he was no good for me. This was not God's will for my life. By then, I was acting out of rebellion. Next the twins of low self-esteem and loneliness rode my shoulder. I started to LOOK FOR LOVE IN ALL THE WRONG PLACES! Despite our differences, despite knowing from the get go that we were unequally yoked, somewhere deep inside I wanted this man to love me. I wanted him to be the one so that I could stop looking. Yeah, I know, I am to be found: "He, who findeth a wife, findeth a good thing..." (Proverbs 18:22). Don't get it twisted, I know the scriptures. I just chose not to apply them at that time (rebellion).

I was tired of meeting people and to find out they were not 'the one.' I knew from day one this man did not have what it took to love me how I should be loved. I knew he would not treat me like I deserve to be treated. But, again, I was looking for love in all the wrong places, in the wrong types of men. I was waiting for them to come and sweep me up from low self-esteem and loneliness. Subconsciously, I thought, surely if I could get someone to love me that would prove to both me and the world that I am lovable because deep inside I had believed Satan's lies that although I was powerful, anointed and had a lot to offer the world, because I had reached a certain age and never married, maybe I was not loveable. Maybe, I was not marriage material. Maybe, I just did not have what it took to be Mrs. Somebody.

Maybe all I had to offer anybody was a prayer. That was the twins: deception and perception having their way. I allowed them to set up strongholds in my mind. I entertained the lie that surely something had to be wrong with Kemberly Elaine since I was what I considered overlooked, too dark, too fat, too rough, too strong, too opinionated, too churchy and definitely not feminine enough: rejection, low self-Esteem, loneliness, self-Sabotage, anger and bitterness all worked together. It did not matter that God reminded me time and time again how fearfully and wonderfully I was made. It did not matter how God reminded me every day how much HE loved me. I was still what I considered old and still went to bed alone at night. Maybe, just maybe, this man with all his craziness could change my lot in life. Just maybe, he can get delivered and saved for real and we could live happily ever after – just maybe...

God makes everything beautiful in its own time. I knew this but it was not enough to fight low self-esteem, loneliness and my flesh at that time. I just wanted to be loved by someone other than my natural family and church members. I had all this love inside of me, waiting to pour out on my mate. What was sad was the man I allowed to come into my world was not even capable of loving me in his present state. We were at two different places spiritually. I knew how to love God, but did not know how to love myself. It appeared from observation he knew how to love himself and that was it. Bottom line is I looked for love from a man that had already let me know from the door he was not in it for the long haul, rather just the game and frills. Do not get caught or stuck like that. When someone tells you or shows you who they are from the start, believe them. When God shows you who He deems you to be, believe Him.

God snatched me out of that situation. Before I came out, I had to deal with each of those spirits one by one. Not only that, I confessed my sins so that I could be healed. I shared with Pastor Stephanie what I was dealing with. I did not give her the details as written in this chapter, but I let her know that I was in a fight for my life and was fornicating. She prayed for me. Although I went back a few times after that, eventually that thing broke in the spirit. When I say it broke, it broke. God was not playing with me. He literally took the taste out of my mouth. I no longer had the desire for him or it. Do not get me wrong, sex is good. That is how God intended for it to be. However, outside of marriage, it is wrong. He kept me and is keeping me. He is a strong tower and deliverer. **You do not have to stay stuck. You have choices and options to move forward.** When you had enough, you do what it takes to come out/get out and stay out.

THOUGHTS TO PONDER

- ❖ Appreciate both your natural and spiritual parents; they have your best interest at heart
- ❖ Do not be moved by distraction and attractions
- ❖ Do not reduce yourself to an arrangement
- ❖ See yourself as God sees you;
- ❖ Know your worth; Do not allow others to determine your value;
- ❖ You too can come out; there is a way of escape
- ❖ The devil does not play fair; he plays for keeps
- ❖ What takes 5 minutes to get into can take 5 years to a life time to get out of
- ❖ Sex outside of marriage IS fornication regardless to who is doing it and says it's okay

NOTES OF INSPIRATION

_____

_____

_____

_____

_____

_____

_____

_____

_____

_____

Chapter 13

BLESSINGS AND BEAUTY

BLESSINGS

My car accident was in 2009. I tried to settle since then. Because I had a horrible attorney who was afraid of State Farm, my accident ended up settling for $1,000. Really? That check just came at the end of 2013 or the beginning of 2014. God told me to sign that check over to my attorney as a payment. I could not believe it. From that car accident, I lost my house and am still stuck in this high car payment and I practically got nothing behind that accident. The young lady driving my car, who had no surgeries, got more than I did. I just could not wrap my brain around that one. It really was not the house so much as it was the settlement in the accident case. That threw me for a loop. However, I have learned through my process to trust God. If He told me to do something it was for a reason. I need not concern myself with the details. It took years to get to that place.

The closure of the accident case and the letter from the attorney about the house all happened around the same time last year. I believe it took me a few months to go through the grieving process. I said I would sue my attorney, but I just did not have the energy to fight that battle. I wanted to put it towards something positive like this book. It took me a minute to K.E.M. but eventually I got to the point where I accepted what God allowed. As I began to let things go. I received healing in my body. My pastor prophesied to me about 2 ½ years ago that God was going to give me a miracle in my leg and that He did.

After having knee problems for 14 years, a diagnosis of arthritis and a recommendation for knee replacement, God healed me. I don't even know when He did it. I just noticed somewhere between January and February, my leg did not bother me going up and down the stairs anymore. I noticed that after shouting in church on a Sunday, I was able to go to work painless in that leg on Monday which had not been the case previously. As I healed emotionally, God healed me physically. Letting it go was worth it. I can even run up to two miles. That was something I have not been able to do since the four knee surgeries. If God makes you a promise, hang in and hold on to it. He is not a man that He should lie. **Do not give up on your dreams or whatever you are believing Him for in your life.**

I sense someone reading this book will think, well you still lost your house. True, I lost my house, but guess what? I was not put out of my house. I walked out of my house and moved my own things out of my house. Then, I got paid to leave the house. Nobody came back to put my stuff out on the lawn again. The reality of it is this; my lender told me this in the midst of me trying to keep the house from foreclosure. He said, "Kem, it's just a material thing. It's just property. That's why they call it real estate. You will get another one." At the time I thought he was just cruel and insensitive, but as I began to let it go, I realized he was right. I am still who God says I am whether owning or renting. Take this disclaimer, I do believe in owning. I know people testify about money and there have been monetary showers of blessings in my life, but I was healed in and by the process. God also brought me out to a wealthy place.

God took me to the story of Joseph and Potiphar's wife. Although Joseph did go to jail because of that situation, she only got his cloak. Joseph could have been stuck on the fact that she got his cloak and ran back for it. Who knows how the story would have ended then. However, she got his cloak, but did not get his integrity. Even then he was being set up for a great comeback. **God knows how to put us in a place and position to activate His favor in our lives. He knows when and who needs a prison experience; not for themselves, but for the sake of others.** He knows how to strategically plant us in the way to be recognized and used even in what we would consider a pitiful situation. The cloak and prison was not the conclusion to Joseph's story. Check it out in Genesis.

I, too, can say like Joseph, "What the enemy intended for my harm, God turned around for my good." Not just in the house and car situation, but in my life. I, too, am like David; it was good that I was afflicted. **I learned that I was not who I thought I was in God, but God is who He says He is in me.** He is Faithful to the end. **I learned that before He could release me as a prophetess to the nations, I had to be healed, delivered and set free. I cannot deliver others and I, myself, am bound up by negativity and stinking thinking about my experiences.** They are just that, experiences. They do not define me although in some instances they were used to shape and guide me.

I am grateful for every pain, trial, testimony, shame, tear, the good, the bad, the ugly and the indifferent. As Paul, I count it all dung. This present suffering is nothing compared to the future glory that shall be revealed in me. I love the Lord. He heard my cry and pitied every groan. As long as I live, when trouble rises, I will haste unto His throne. Regardless of what I endured, I survived. I made it. **Although in it, it may have seemed like the death of me, but it certainly was not the end of me.** It was just that, the death of me. I die daily for the sake of the cross. My birth certificate was a death certificate.

Now I am writing this book to snatch somebody else out of the grave, out of the pit, out of depression, out of a place called stuck. You cannot stay there. God has work for you to do. He has a purpose and a plan for your life. He also has a purpose and plan for your pain. There is somebody counting on you, waiting on you to get yourself together so that you can reach back and grabbed them. **Do not abort your assignment. Do not give your gifts, talents and potential to the grave.** There is no use for them there. God put them in you for use on this earth. If you die before you reach your destiny, all that is within you dies with you and is for naught.

Get up and take off those grave clothes. Take up your bed and walk. Dare to walk on water. **Walk over what had you drowning.** God is your very present help in the time of trouble. Greater is He that is in you than he that is in the world. I can truly say that I would have fainted had I not believed to see God's goodness in the land of the living. I admonish you to wait on the Lord, be of good courage as He strengthens your heart (Psalms 27:13-14).

When I say God did the work in me; He did the work in me. I truly love myself now. I am okay with myself. As badly as I wanted to be married and have my twins by now, I can honestly say without regret, bitterness, anger, rejection, low self-esteem and all the other spirits that I was dealing with internally that, if I get married, I do; and if I don't, I don't; God Bless. **God is still God regardless and life is worth the living irrespectively.** Not only did God take the pain of my past away, He took away the stigma and sting of being single. So what if I am unmarried?

I realized that I had conformed to what society deemed as okay: married with children, 2 acres and a mule. I felt that I was rejected because I was not married. But it has never been about being single or married. It was about being chosen. I have been chosen by God to serve Him. While I am single, my cares are of Him. That is what is important; and that is all that matters. I am content with who I am, where I am and whose I am. **I do not need a status to be accepted.** I am the beloved of God and that settles it. Because of that, God can use me and trust me now to minister to children and families across the world.

In November 2009, both Pastor Stephanie and Apostle Jennings said that year, 2010 was going to be Divine Order. Pastor Stephanie said that there would be a shift in our humility because we will need it where God is taking us. Where God is taking us, pride cannot stay but humility will keep us. She also said that there would be a shift in our desires. Apostle Jennings said that in 2010 we would shift out of church age and into kingdom. 2010 would be a season of balance and maturity. After years of pain, problems and perplexity, God is bringing stability and order and that we are getting ready to be anointed with kingdom power. He said that in 2010 there will be a prophetic navigation. God has anointed us to do more than what we are doing and that we must get rid of fear and failure... Thy Kingdom come.

On Thursday, November 19, 2009, Apostle Jennings told us to leap into the blessing that God had for us in 2010. I literally leaped. Little did I know that in May, 2010, I would leap on a plane headed to South Africa for my first international mission's trip. What is ironic about this is, I never had a desire to go to Africa. I did not want to have anything to do with Africa. As a child, I was teased about my dark complexion. My brother had a nickname for me T.B. (Tar Bear). It hurt my feelings every time he or someone in the neighborhood called me that. Do not worry; I am healed from all of that. My brother and I love each other immensely. I hated black history month because they always wanted me to dress as a slave or play Harriet Tubman. I was not comfortable with the way I looked when I was dressed like that. Because I had keen features, people already thought I was from Africa anyway. All the foreign men wanted to talk to me. It was hard getting an American born boyfriend. Needless to say, Africa was never my desire.

However, not my will but Thine will be done. I had no idea that the trip to South Africa would catapult me a step towards destiny. What is even more ironic is that back in 1995 while living in Philadelphia, I babysat my pastor's son while he and his wife went to Africa. He came back and shared with the congregation their experience and even talked of planning a church trip. People were excited about going. However, I told him not me... NEVER. 1) I hate flying and you will never get me on a plane that long. 2) I was black enough and did not need to go to Africa to get any darker. But, I leaped!

I even told my pastor that somebody had to stay back interceding on their behalves to make sure the plane landed safely to and fro. Fifteen years later, a word was spoken, I received it and it launched me into my destiny. God pricked my heart and I leaped into one of the most amazing blessings I have ever had in my life. I accepted the call to go to Cape Town, South Africa. I would not have been able to receive of the Lord with all that junk in my heart/spirit.

Although my co-worker and I started working at the same school in 2006, it was not until 2010 that we would have a conversation about him being from South Africa and his church traveling there to do missions. To be honest, I thought he was Hispanic although he looked like he was Arabian. His name was Ashwin Lewis. There was nothing African about that name to me. As we talked, he shared about the trip and how God used and brought him all the way to America on a teacher program. Little did he know that he would attend and later join, Briarlake Baptist Church. God used Ashwin to make the connection from North America to South Africa.

As he was telling me his story, I felt a leap in my belly. I was not sure what it was at that time, but I was certain it had nothing to do with going to South Africa. No way; not me. As I was traveling home that afternoon, I felt a tug in my spirit. I just began to tell the Lord yes. I was not sure at the moment what the "yes" was for, but I knew God was birthing something in me at that very moment. I pulled over to the side of the road, and as tears stream down my face, I continue to cry, "Yes." God loves ministering to me in my car! I talk about that high car payment, but that car is highly anointed. Anyway, I said, "Lord, I want to go." Then the Steve Urkel came out in me and I said to myself, "Did I say that?" But again I said, "Lord I want to go to Cape Town, South Africa." I cried all the way home. I could not believe it. I was so excited. I could not sleep that night. I just kept praising God the entire evening.

The next morning, I was up early for devotions and arrived to work early. That was a first that school year. I was never early; barely on time. Anyway, I ran to Ashwin's classroom. He was not there. I could not believe it. The one morning I was on time/early, he was late. I kept running down to his classroom to see if he had made it to work. Finally, as the bell rang, he arrived. I ran to him all excited. I felt like Elizabeth when Mary came to visit her. I said, "Ashwin, Ashwin, I want to go on the trip to South Africa with you. You think your church will allow me to go?"

He said, "I was telling my wife, Kemberly would be good for this trip." I went to my pastor one Wednesday after Bible study and told him about the trip. I told him I was interested in going. He told me to get more information and get back with him. Meanwhile, Ashwin had gotten permission for me to travel with his local assembly. I attended the interest meeting. The rest is history. From then on, I spent the next 4 summers traveling to Cape Town, South Africa.

My church partnered with Briarlake Baptist Church and in our four-year travel span each year we conducted a Bible-based day camp for approximately 500-800 children, grades k-6, hosted Block Parties and participated in other missions and evangelical activities in underdeveloped areas in that region. In addition to that, each year The Harvest Tabernacle Church distributed enough groceries to feed over 250 children and their families for at least 4 weeks. The Harvest coat drive raised enough money to purchase coats for over 300 children (ages birth to 15 years of age). I was able to personally lead a team of seven, including my pastor, to Cape Town. I was called to Georgia for such a time as this. **The devil wanted me to abort my mission.** Fortunately he failed because my times are in God's hands.

I use to question, why me Lord? Why am I always going through things? Why do I have to always look crazy? Why do I always struggle? He said if I want to reign with Him, I have to suffer with Him. He said, you gave Me permission to get the Glory out of your life. **It is in Me that you live, move and have your being.** Most importantly, I knew that I could trust you. I knew that Kemberly Elaine McKenzie would be able to walk on and over what others drowned in. He reminded me that **at no time, did He put more on me than I could bear.** I am built to last. I am made in His image. I am a mover and shaker. I have lives to touch, and nations to reach.

"The Spirit of the Lord is upon me because He has anointed me to preach the gospel to the poor; He hath sent me to heal the broken hearted, to preach deliverance to the captives and recovering of sight to the blind, to set at liberty them that are bruised, to preach the acceptable year of the Lord" (Luke 4:18-19).

That is my assignment, what about you? Who would have known that God had all that in store for me? Cape Town was just the beginning. It was not the apex of my purpose here on earth. I have not even scratched the surface. I just know that I am willing, able and available for all that God has for me. His plan is to prosper us and bring us to an expected end. However, you have to move past stuck whatever that is for you. Mine was facing my past and ultimately myself. Yours may be the same or you may have to face others. Whatever you have to face, face it so that you can K.E.M...Keep moving towards purpose and destiny.

BEAUTY

One thing I have accepted through all of this is: "Beauty lies within the eyes of the beholder." Whoever is starring at an object or person determines its beauty. Therefore, if you think you are beautiful then you are. So when we think about ourselves according to the Word of God, we are fearfully and wonderfully made. David looked at himself and told God that we are fearfully and wonderfully made – Marvelous is God's work. Therefore, behold God's works, creation, us, the universe and say, humans, fearfully made. "How precious also are thy thoughts unto me O God! How great is the sum of them!" (Psalms 139:17). The thoughts God has towards me/us cannot be counted. They are more than the sand. Can you name or pick one beach and count the sand?

When I go to sleep and awake you are still thinking about me/us (vs.18). Search me O Lord, and know my heart and see if there be any wicked way in me, and lead me in the way everlasting. To sum this up,

If the word says that I am fearfully and wonderfully made, then that is how I need to see myself since beauty lies within my eyes (the eyes of the beholder). If I do not see myself according to God's Word, then I need God to search my heart and remove whatever is contrary to His Word. The light of the body is the eye: therefore, when thine eye is single, thy whole body also is full of light; but when thine eye is evil, thy body also is full of darkness (Luke 11:34). Check your vision.

We must also learn to get God's perspective from the place where He is. From there, mountains look like molehills. It is imperative that we change our viewpoint (perception). If we look at stuff from an earthly realm, then we are not high enough. Our Father who art in heaven (John 17). Instead of seeing how big the storm is; tell the storm how big your God is.

Do not allow your past mistakes, failures, mishaps and misunderstandings to keep you from being all that you can be. True it happened, yes it hurt, but your past or present circumstance(s) are not your final conclusion. You are not your past. Of course, we use our past to get to our present and as a guide to our future, but we learn from it, not stay stuck in it. I am not just talking about negative experiences either, some people stay stuck on their last victory. Great, celebrate it, but learn to K.E.M. (Keep Everything Moving). It is time to make a move toward complete wholeness. Life is all about reconciliation between God, ourselves and others. It is time to make amends.

THOUGHTS TO PONDER

❖ There is an expiration date on your trouble
❖ When God delivers, you do not go back or look back
❖ Leave old play mates and play grounds alone
❖ God declared the end from the beginning
❖ Do not despise small beginnings
❖ It is time to stop dating God and marry Him
❖ Always keep a nevertheless in your spirit
❖ Now's the time to start the healing process
❖ God will heal you everywhere you hurt
❖ Destiny awaits you, now go.
❖ (K.E.M.) KEEP EVERYTHING MOVING

NOTES OF INSPIRATION

_____
_____
_____
_____
_____
_____
_____
_____
_____
_____

ABOUT THE AUTHOR

Dr. Kemberly Elaine McKenzie was born in Washington, D.C. and reared in Takoma Park, MD. She graduated from High Point High School in Prince Georges County, MD. Her thirst for knowledge forced her to obtain a bachelor's, three masters and a Ph.D. She earned a B.A. in Communications; a M.Ed. in Elementary Education; M.S. in Special Education; an M.A. and Ph.D. in Educational Leadership. She attended the following colleges: Harrisburg Area Community College – Harrisburg, Pa; Messiah College – Grantham, PA; Temple University, Philadelphia, PA; Eastern Baptist Theological Seminary – Wynnewood, PA; Cheyney State University – Cheyney, PA; Chicago State University, Chicago, IL; and Capella University – St. Paul, MN. Dr. McKenzie was also afforded the opportunity to study abroad at The University of Cambridge in London, England.

As an educator, Dr. McKenzie has 18 years of teaching experience; 14 of which have been devoted to special education. She is National Board Certified in Special Education. She is a behavior specialist and enjoys working with at-risk youth. She is a writer. Her poetry has appeared in the Philadelphia Inquirer. As a motivational speaker, she has offered several professional and staff development trainings and workshops on the importance of adding humor to your everyday life.

Her dissertation was entitled, *Teacher Burnout: A Laughing Matter.* She has the gift of exhortation and loves to make people laugh.

As a missionary, Dr. McKenzie has over 30 years serving in nursing homes, shelters, hospitals and other non-profit organization such as The Salvation Army and Habitat for Humanity. Dr. McKenzie has traveled extensively around the world. She travels out of the United States to service children and family in underdeveloped countries, such as Cape Town, South Africa. She enjoys working with and ministering to the underprivileged populations and teens at risk. Her motto in life is, 'If I can help somebody as I travel along life's way; then my living will not be in vain.'

Dr. McKenzie enjoys taking pictures and has a photography company: Higher Dimensions Photography. She wears many hats. She is a licensed and ordained minister, missionary, educator, motivational speaker, behavior specialist and author. She enjoys many hobbies such as sports, crocheting, playing musical instruments, writing songs and playing games. Most importantly, Dr. McKenzie loves family and loves to laugh.

Dr. McKenzie was once at a place called stuck herself which inspired the movement, K.E.M. (Keep Everything Moving). She learned to allow adversity to push her towards destiny. She desires to inspire and push others to reach their fullest potential. She understands that before you move forward, you have to turn backwards and deal face to face with whatever is holding you captive. Dr. McKenzie shares her story in belief that others will be encouraged to celebrate adversity on their way to destiny.

For speaking engagements and book signings, her contact information is www.kemberlymckenzie.com

CPSIA information can be obtained
at www.ICGtesting.com
Printed in the USA
FSOW03n0425260917
39175FS